จะเข้
jà-khêh
**crocodile-shaped
fretted floor zither**

ดอกมะลิ
dàwk má-lí
**jasmine
blossoms**

ชานมเย็น
chaa-nom-yen
Thai Milk Tea

ผัดกะเพราหมู
phàt gà-phrao mǔu
Minced pork with sweet basil

T0021525

สุโขทัย
sù-khǒh-thai
Sukhothai Temple

**The free online audio recordings for this book
may be downloaded as follows:**

Type the following URL into your web browser:
www.tuttlepublishing.com/Thai-Picture-Dictionary
For support, email us at info@tuttlepublishing.com

THAI
PICTURE
DICTIONARY

LEARN 1,500 THAI WORDS AND EXPRESSIONS

Jintana Rattanakhemakorn

TUTTLE Publishing

Tokyo | Rutland, Vermont | Singapore

Contents

A Basic Introduction to Thai

This dictionary aims to help you learn the simple and practical Thai vocabulary that people actually use at work, at home, and in everyday situations. In this book you will find 38 practical lessons with more than 1,500 common Thai words and phrases. Each section contains 25–35 words and also has five to eight sentences demonstrating the usage of these words. The words and sentences in the dictionary all appear in the following order: Thai script, followed by the romanized pronunciation and then the English meaning. Every item is part of the functional vocabulary that learners need to use in daily life and to qualify for language competence when working in Thailand.

Overview of the Thai language

Standard Thai, also known as Central Thai, is the official national language of Thailand. It is the native language of around eighty percent of the population of the country and is used as a medium of instruction in schools, in the media and in all government affairs. There are three other major dialects: southern, northern and northeastern. These dialects are not used at school and in a university setting. Therefore, Thai people do not expect foreigners to be able to speak these dialects.

The origins of the Thai script can be traced back to a south Indian script which was introduced into mainland Southeast Asia during the 4th or 5th century AD. However, the written Thai language derives from the Old Khmer alphabet and was instituted by the third Sukothai period king, Ramkamhaeng, in 1283. This writing system is based on Pali, Sanskrit, and other Indian models. Thai, like other Indian-based scripts, lists consonants and vowels separately.

The Thai script has some complex rules regarding pronunciation. As in English, because the language has changed over time, multiple letters often represent the same sounds.On the other hand, the sounds of many Thai letters vary depending on whether they occur at the beginning or at the end of a syllable.

Thai Consonants

Below is a chart showing the basic Thai alphabet. There are 44 letters including 21 initial consonant sounds and 8 ending consonant sounds.

Consonant Form	Consonant Sound	Sounds like	Thai Example
ก	g	g as in get	กับ gàp
ข ค ฆ	kh	k as in kind	ขาย khǎay
ง	ng	ng as in singing	เงิน ngerrn
จ	j	j as in joy	ใจ jai
ฉ ช ฌ	ch	ch as in chair	ชอบ châwp
ซ ศ ษ ส	s	s as in sand	สอน sǎwn
ญ ย	y	y as in yes	ยาย yaay
ฎ ด	d	d as in dog	ได้ dâi
ฏ ต	t	t as in stand	ตอน tawn

Consonant Form	Consonant Sound	Sounds like	Thai Example
ฐ ฑ ฒ ถ ท ธ	th	t as in **teach**	ทำ **th**am
ณ น	n	n as in **need**	นอน **n**awn
บ	b	ɔ as in s**p**in	บ่าย **b**àay
ป	p	ɔ as in s**p**in	ปี **p**ii
ผ พ ภ	ph	ɔ as in **p**ost	พี่ **ph**îi
ฝ ฟ	f	f as in **f**un	ฟัง **f**ang
ม	m	m as in **m**ore	แม่ **m**âeh
ร	r	r as in **r**un	ร้อย **r**óy
ล ฬ	l	l as in **l**ong	เล่น **l**êhn
ว	w	w as in **w**hen	วัน **w**an
ห ฮ	h	h as in **h**ave	ห้า **h**âa
*อ	*a/e/i/o/u	o as in **o**ut	อ้วน **ô**uan

*Note: The letter 'อ' acts as a silent vowel carrier (a/e/i/o/u) at the beginning of words that start with a vowel.

Ending Consonants

Below is a list of eight consonant sounds appearing at the end of a syllable. When these consonants appear at the end of a word, they are not voiced aloud but are silent.

Consonant sound	Sounds like	Thai Example
k	k/g as in pi**ck**/hu**g**	มาก màa**k**
t	d/t as in lou**d**/hi**t**	ลด ló**t**
p	b/p as in lo**b**/ca**p**	กลับ glà**p**
ng	ng as in wro**ng**	สอง sǎw**ng**
n	n as in ca**n**	หวาน wǎa**n**
m	m as in di**m**	ลม lo**m**
y	y as in bu**y**	สวย sǔa**y**
w	w as in lo**w**	ข้าว khâa**w**

Vowels

Thai has a complicated set of vowels and diphthongs (combinations of two vowels). There are 18 single vowels, which are generally separated into short and long forms. Plus, there are three dipthongs and three additional vowels which are considered to be long vowels. When speaking of "long" and "short" vowels, we refer to the length of time the vowel is pronounced. For example, a "long vowel" is 'naaaa', where the "a" sound is drawn out for a long duration.

1. Short vowels

Vowel sound	Sounds like	Thai Example
a	u as in hut	คะ khá
i	i as in kid	สิ sì
ue	um as in rhythm	รึ rúe
u	u as in put	จุ jù
e	e as in let (shorter)	เบะ bè
ae	a as in hat (shorter)	แกะ gàe
o	o as in oh! (shorter)	โละ pò
aw	o as in shot	เจาะ jàw
er	ur as in blur (shorter)	เลอะ lér

2. Long vowels

Vowel sound	Sounds like	Thai Example
aa	ar as in bar	ขา khăa
ii	ee as in tree	มี mii
ueh	eu as in "ü" in German (longer)	ถือ thŭeh
uu	oo as in good	ดู duu
eh	ay as in pay	เซ seh
aeh	air as in hair	แห hăeh
oh	ow as in show	โต toh
aw	aw as in saw	ขอ khăw
err	er as in her	เจอ jerr

3. Dipthongs and extra vowels

Vowel sound	Sounds like	Thai Example
ua	ur as in tour	กลัว glua
ia	ea as hear	เสีย sĭa
uea	ua as in dual (longer)	เสือ sŭea
am	um as in dump	ดำ dam
ai	ie as in die	ไป pai
ao	ous as in house	เขา khăo

Tones

Tones are an essential element of the Thai language. Standard Thai has five tones—**mid**, **low**, **falling**, **high**, and **rising**. Every Thai word has a particular tone assigned to it and these tones help to distinguish the meaning of one word from another—which means that many different words have similar pronunciations except for the tones, which are different. Tones can change the meaning of words—for example the word for "close" becomes "far", and "pretty" becomes "bad luck" when pronounced with a different tone. Below is a chart showing the tones and examples of how words with the same sound can take on different meanings when the tone changes.

Tone	Symbol	Example	Meaning
mid	no mark	ปา paa	throw
low	ˋ	ป่า pàa	forest, jungle
falling	ˆ	ป้า pâa	aunt (mother's older sister)
high	´	ป๊า páa	an informal term to call father, derived from Chinese
rising	ˇ	ป๋า pǎa	an informal term to call father, derived from Chinese

The following is a chart illustrating how Thai tones work. Please listen to the audio recordings to familiarize yourself with the five different tones.

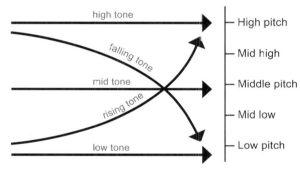

- A high tone is pronounced with a high level pitch.
- A falling tone starts high and drops at the end.
- A mid tone is produced in a constant pitch in the normal vocal range.
- A rising tone starts low and the pitch goes up at the end.
- A low tone is level and lower than the normal range.

Basic Thai Grammar

Thai grammar is very simple and straightforward. You can easily formulate sentences by following the same word order as in English. Here are some basic rules to help you understand the Thai sentence structure.
- Thai basic sentence word order is **subject + verb + object** like English.
- In order to form a question, you add a short question word at the end of the sentence, which is like a verbal question mark.

*Khun mii phîi náwng **mái?***	Do you have brothers and sisters?
*Khun phûut phaa-sǎa **à-rai?***	What is your mother tongue?

- No articles like "a", "an" or "the" are used in Thai.
- There are no plural forms.
- Thai verbs do not change and have only one simple form regardless of subject or tense. For example, "to go" is the same whether the subject is I, you, he/she or they, and whether the action took place in the past, present or future. So, Thai words never change form.
- Tenses are indicated by using a "timeframe" or helping words at the beginning or the end of the sentence. In order to state the past or the future in Thai, you can use the following optional words.

    1. Time words, such as now, today, yesterday, tomorrow, six o'clock, etc. For example,

Wan-níi *chăn mâi sà-baay.*	Today I'm not feeling well.
Phrûng níi *phŏm wâang.*	I'm free tomorrow.

    2. Using "**láew**" แล้ว (already) at the very end of the sentence to indicate that something has been completed before or prior to the moment of speaking. For example,

*Chăn gin yaa **láew**.*	I've already taken medicine.
*Phŏm khâo-jai **láew**.*	I already understood.

    3. Using "**jà**" จะ (will) in front of a verb to indicate the future sometimes with a time word added to emphasize when it is going to happen in the future. For example,

*Wan săo-aa-thít khun **jà** tham à-rai?*	What will you do on weekends?
*Chăn **jà** jàay ngerrn-sòt.*	I will pay in cash.

- Different Thai personal pronouns are used for males and females. However, the same pronouns are used for subject and object (there's no difference between 'I' and 'me' or 'he/she' and 'him/her'). The commonly used personal pronouns are:

English Pronoun	Thai Pronoun
I, me	*phŏm* (for male speakers)
I, me	*chăn* (for female speakers)
you (polite)	*khun*
he, she, they	*khăo*
we, us	*rao*

    Note: In casual conversation, it's very common to omit the subject, especially "I" and "You". Also, a nickname is often used to refer to yourself or a third person rather than using a personal pronoun.
- Each object has a special classifier word that should be used when stating a quantity of that object. A simple rule is **noun** + **number** + **classifier** i.e., "**paper** + **four** + **sheets**" = four sheets of paper (= *grà-dàat sìi phàaen*) or "**wine** + **three** + **bottles**" = three bottles of wine (= *waii săam khùat*).
- Thai adjectives can function as verbs without adding any form of the verb "to be" simply by placing the adjective after the noun, as in the following examples.

    The flower is beautiful = **Flower** + **beautiful** = *dàwk mái sŭay*
- No punctuation is used to indicate a question or the end of a Thai sentence.

Another key aspect of Thai for non-native speakers is the use of polite gender-specific particles. These are used to indicate politeness, respect and courtesy at the end of a sentence.
- Women say *khâ* (with a falling tone) when making a statement and also alone as a polite way to reply "yes." But at the end of a question, they use *khá* (with a high tone).
- Men generally use the word *khráp* as a polite ending in every situation.

These respectful particles are not translatable. However, it is recommended to add them whenever you speak or reply to any Thai person you have just met or do not know well. It is best to use these polite endings both in formal and casual speech.

Thai Greetings

When greeting someone, Thai people normally say *sà-wàt-dii khâ* (women) or *sà-wàt-dii khráp* (men) for "hi," "good morning," "good afternoon," or "good evening." People perform the *wâi*, the traditional form of Thai greeting, when saying this. The proper way to do the *wâi* is to make a slight bow with the palms pressed together. The *wâi* is not just for greetings or paying respects, it also expresses goodbye, gratitude or an apology.

When someone gives the *wâi* to you, you should always return the *wâi* as a sign of respect. Buddhist monks do not have to do so as they are considered representatives of the Buddha.

Names and Titles

Nicknames are very commonly used in Thailand. Thais often tell you their nickname instead of their first name. First given names are mainly used for very formal situations and written communications only.

In order to address a person you don't know well and meet for the first time, the title *Khun* should always be used before the given name in the same way that we would use Mr, Mrs, or Ms and for men or women, married or single. Family names are rarely used, only first names preceded by *khun*. For example, **Kanya** (given name) + **Rakdee** (family name) becomes **Khun Kanya** in speech and correspondence. If you don't know their names, you can simply address someone as **Khun**.

How to use this Dictionary

First of all, for the self-study learner, it is best to begin by learning the romanized consonant and vowel sounds together with the tone markings so that you can understand how to pronounce each sound correctly. Next, choose your topics of interest and read through the vocabulary on that page. Practice pronouncing the words in context with the conversations and phrases provided while listening to the recordings so that you memorize the words with the correct pronunciation and tone.

Here are a few tips on how to practice with this picture dictionary

- Listen to the audio recordings several times and say the Thai words aloud as you look at the pictures. Repeating them over and over again can help you build up your memory of the vocabulary and phrases.
- This picture dictionary should be appropriate for beginners to learn spoken Thai, not reading and writing. However, if you want to go beyond basic Thai, then you should start learning the Thai script.

The free online audio recordings for this book may be downloaded as follows:

Type the following URL into your web browser:
www.tuttlepublishing.com/Thai-Picture-Dictionary
For support, email us at info@tuttlepublishing.com

ยินดีที่ได้รู้จัก

Yin-dii thîi dâi rúu-jàk

So nice to meet you!

1 สวัสดีค่ะ สบายดีไหมคะ
Sà-wàt-dii khâ, sà-baay dii mái khá?
Hello, how are you?

2 ผมสบายดีครับ ขอบคุณครับ
Phǒm sà-baay dii khráp, khàwp-khun khráp!
I am fine, thank you!

3 พบ; เจอ
phóp (formal); jerr (informal)
to meet

8 อะไร
à-rai
what?

9 ดีใจ
dii-jai
satisfied

10 มีความสุข
mii khwaam-sùk
happy

11 สนุก
sà-nùk
joyful

4 จินดา นี่คุณวิชัยครับ
Jinda, nîi khun Wichai khráp.
Jinda, this is Wichai.

5 สวัสดีค่ะ
Sà-wàt-dii khâ.
Hello.

6 ยินดีที่ได้รู้จักครับ
Yin-dii thîi dâi rúu-jàk khráp!
Pleased to meet you!

7 แนะนำ
náe-nam
to introduce

12 เรียก
rîak
**to call;
to be called**

13 ไหว้
wâi
the traditional greeting of Thailand

15 สวัสดีครับ ผมชื่อ สมิธ คุณชื่ออะไรครับ
Sà-wàt-dii khráp. Phǒm chûeh Smith. Khun chûeh à-rai khráp?
Hi, my name is Smith. What's your name?

16 ฉันชื่อกันยา นามสกุลรักดี นี่นามบัตรของฉันค่ะ
Chǎn chûeh Kanya, naam-sà-gun Rakdee. Nîi naam-bàt khawng chǎn khâ.
My first name is Kanya, surname is Rakdee. Here's my namecard.

14 แนะนำตัว
náe-nam tua
introduce yourself

17 สวัสดีครับ! แล้วเจอกัน
Sà-wàt-dii khráp! Láehw jerr gan!
Goodbye! See you!

18 โชคดี
Chôhk-dii!
Good luck!

Additional Vocabulary

23 ชื่อ
chûeh
name

24 นามสกุล
naam-sà-gun
surname

25 คุณ
khun
you

26 รู้
rúu
to know

27 เชื้อชาติ
chúea châat
nationality

28 เชคแฮนด์
chéhk haehn
shake hands

29 กอด
gàwt
to hug

30 จูบ
jùup
to kiss

31 ยิ้ม
yím
smile

32 โบกมือ
bòhk mueh
wave

33 โค้งคำนับ
khóhng kham-náp
to bow

34 ทักทาย
thák-thaay
to greet

35 ชวนคุย
chuan khui
to start a conversation

36 พูดคุยสั้นๆ
phûut khui sân sân
to make small talk

37 คุยเล่น; นินทา
khui lêhn; nin-thaa
to chat; to gossip

38 เป็นยังไงบ้าง
Pen yang-ngai bâang?
How are things?

39 ทำไม
Tham-mai?
Why?

40 เพื่อน
phûean
friends

19 รวมกลุ่ม; พบปะ
ruam glum; phóp pà
gathering; meeting

20 ลูกค้า
lúuk kháa
guest; customer

21 ขอบคุณ
Khàwp-khun!
Thank you!

22 ไม่เป็นไร
Mâi-pen-rai.
Not at all.

2

ครอบครัวของฉัน/ผม
Khrâwp-khrua khăwng chăn/phŏm
My family

Additional Vocabulary

1 ลูกชาย *lûuk chaay* **son**	**2** ผู้ชาย *phûu chaay* **male**	**3** ผู้หญิง *phûu yǐng* **female**

5 ลูกสาว
lûuk săaw
daughter

4 ลูก
lûuk
children

6 พ่อแม่
phâw mâeh
parents

26 ภรรยา
phan-yaa
wife

27 สามี
săa-mii
husband

28 อา
aa
father's younger brother/sister

29 ป้า
pâa
father's older sister

30 ลุง
lung
mother's elder brother

31 ลูกเขย
lûuk-khŏei
son-in-law

32 ลูกสะใภ้
lûuk sà-phái
daughter-in-law

33 หลานชาย;
หลานสาว
lăan-săaw;
lăan chaay
grandson;
granddaughter

34 ญาติ
yâat
relatives

35 เพื่อนบ้าน
phûean bâan
neighbor

36 น้องเขย; พี่เขย
náwng-khŏei;
phîi-khŏei
brother-in-law

37 น้องสะใภ้;
พี่สะใภ้
náwng sà-phái;
phîi sà-phái
sister-in-law

38 ครอบครัว
khrâwp-khrua
family

39 ตัวเอง
tua-ehng
self

40 อายุน้อย
aa-yú náwy
young

41 กระตือรือร้น
grà-tueh-rueh-rón
enthusiastic

42 เชื่อ
chûea
to believe

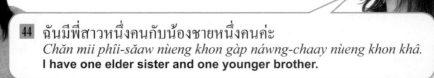

43 คุณมีพี่น้องกี่คน
Khun mii phîi náwng gìi khon?
How many brothers and sisters do you have?

44 ฉันมีพี่สาวหนึ่งคนกับน้องชายหนึ่งคนค่ะ
Chăn mii phîi-săaw nùeng khon gàp náwng-chaay nùeng khon khâ.
I have one elder sister and one younger brother.

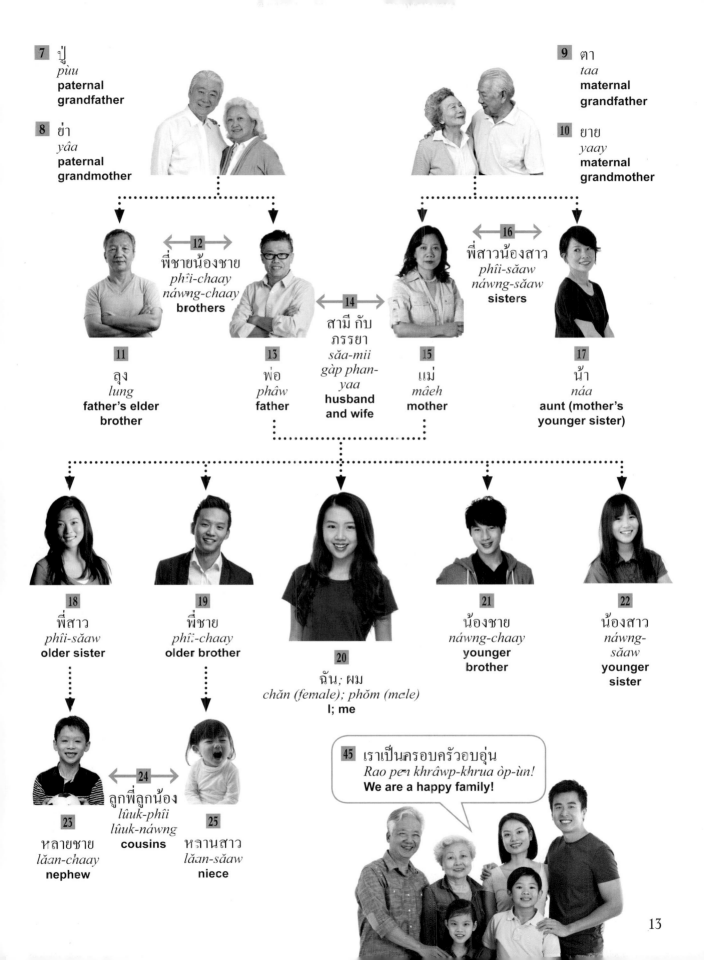

7 ปู่
pùu
paternal grandfather

8 ย่า
yâa
paternal grandmother

9 ตา
taa
maternal grandfather

10 ยาย
yaay
maternal grandmother

12 พี่ชายน้องชาย
phîi-chaay náwng-chaay
brothers

16 พี่สาวน้องสาว
phîi-săaw náwng-săaw
sisters

14 สามี กับ ภรรยา
săa-mii gàp phan-yaa
husband and wife

11 ลุง
lung
father's elder brother

13 พ่อ
phâw
father

15 แม่
mâeh
mother

17 น้า
náa
aunt (mother's younger sister)

18 พี่สาว
phîi-săaw
older sister

19 พี่ชาย
phîi-chaay
older brother

20 ฉัน; ผม
chăn (female); phŏm (male)
I; me

21 น้องชาย
náwng-chaay
younger brother

22 น้องสาว
náwng-săaw
younger sister

24 ลูกพี่ลูกน้อง
lûuk-phîi lûuk-náwng
cousins

23 หลายชาย
lăan-chaay
nephew

25 หลานสาว
lăan-săaw
niece

45 เราเป็นครอบครัวอบอุ่น
Rao pen khrâwp-khrua òp-ùn!
We are a happy family!

บ้านของฉัน/ผม

3

Bâan khăwng chăn/phŏm

My house

№	ไทย	คำอ่าน	English
1	ห้องนั่งเล่น	*hâwng nâng lêhn*	living room
2	ระเบียง	*rá-biang*	balcony
3	ราวระเบียง	*raaw rá-biang*	railing
4	เพดาน	*pheh-daan*	ceiling
5	กุญแจ	*gun-jaeh*	keys
6	ภาพวาด	*phâap wâat*	painting
7	โคมไฟ	*khohm-fai*	lamp
8	เก้าอี้	*gâo-îi*	chair
9	กำแพง	*gam-phaehng*	wall
10	โทรทัศน์; ทีวี	*thoh-rá-thát* (formal); *thii-wii* (informal)	television
11	โต๊ะกาแฟ	*tó gaa-faeh*	coffee table
12	พรม	*phrom*	carpet

№	ไทย	คำอ่าน	English
13	แอร์	*aeh*	air conditioner
14	โต๊ะ	*tó*	table
15	โซฟา	*soh-faa*	sofa
16	พื้น	*phúehn*	floor
17	ผ้าม่าน	*phâa-mâan*	curtain
18	หน้าต่าง	*nâa-tàang*	window
19	หมอน	*măwn*	pillow
20	เตียง	*tiang*	bed
21	ห้องนอน	*hâwng nawn*	bedroom
22	ห้อง	*hâwng*	room

Additional Vocabulary

№	ไทย	คำอ่าน	English
49	สวิตช์ไฟ	*sà-wít fai*	light switch
50	ปลั๊กไฟ	*plák fai*	electric socket; power point
51	บ้าน	*bâan*	house
52	อพาร์ทเมนท์	*à-pháat-méhn*	apartment
53	หลังคา	*lăng-khaa*	roof
54	ห้องใต้หลังคา	*hâwng tâi lăng-khaa*	attic; loft
55	ห้องใต้ดิน	*hâwng tâi din*	basement; cellar
56	โรงรถ	*rohng rót*	garage

57 บ้านสวยมากเลย ฉัน/ผมอยากอยู่ที่นี่
Bâan sŭay mâak loei. Chăn/Phŏm yàak yùu thîi nîi.
What a beautiful house. I would love to live here.

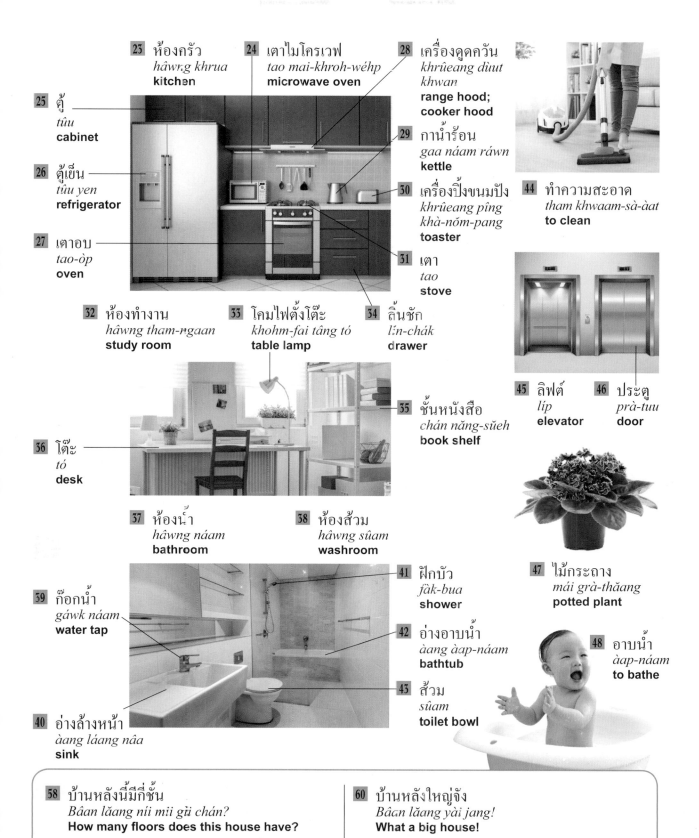

23 ห้องครัว
hâwng khrua
kitchen

24 เตาไมโครเวฟ
tao mai-khroh-wéhp
microwave oven

28 เครื่องดูดควัน
khrûeang dùut khwan
range hood; cooker hood

25 ตู้
tûu
cabinet

29 กาน้ำร้อน
gaa náam ráwn
kettle

26 ตู้เย็น
tûu yen
refrigerator

30 เครื่องปิ้งขนมปัง
khrûeang pîng khà-nóm-pang
toaster

44 ทำความสะอาด
tham khwaam-sà-àat
to clean

27 เตาอบ
tao-òp
oven

31 เตา
tao
stove

32 ห้องทำงาน
hâwng tham-ngaan
study room

33 โคมไฟตั้งโต๊ะ
khohm-fai tâng tó
table lamp

34 ลิ้นชัก
lín-chák
drawer

35 ชั้นหนังสือ
chán năng-sŭeh
book shelf

45 ลิฟต์
líp
elevator

46 ประตู
prà-tuu
door

36 โต๊ะ
tó
desk

37 ห้องน้ำ
hâwng náam
bathroom

38 ห้องส้วม
hâwng sûam
washroom

41 ฝักบัว
fàk-bua
shower

47 ไม้กระถาง
mái grà-thăang
potted plant

39 ก๊อกน้ำ
gáwk náam
water tap

42 อ่างอาบน้ำ
àang àap-náam
bathtub

43 ส้วม
sûam
toilet bowl

48 อาบน้ำ
àap-náam
to bathe

40 อ่างล้างหน้า
àang láang nâa
sink

---

58 บ้านหลังนี้มีกี่ชั้น
Bâan lăng níi mii gìi chán?
How many floors does this house have?

60 บ้านหลังใหญ่จัง
Bâan lăng yài jang!
What a big house!

59 ฉัน/ผมอยากเช่าอพาร์ทเมนท์
Chăn/Phŏm yàak cháo à-pháat-méhn.
I would like to rent an apartment.

61 ฉัน/ผมอยากดูห้องครัว
Chăn/Phŏm yàak duu hâwng khrua.
I want to see the kitchen.

15

4

ร่างกาย
Râang-gaay
The human body

1 หัว
hǔa
head

2 หู
hǔu
ear

3 คอ
khaw
neck

6 ผม
phǒm
hair

7 คิ้ว
khíw
eyebrow

8 ตา
taa
eye

9 จมูก
jà-mùuk
nose

10 ปาก
pàak
mouth

4 แก้ม
gâehm
cheek

5 หน้า
nâa
face

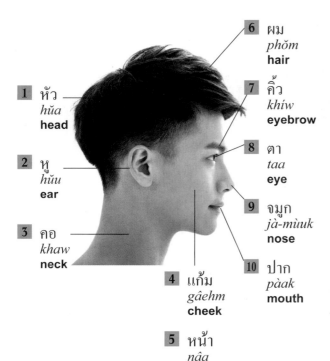

11 ลิ้น
lín
tongue

12 ฟัน
fan
teeth

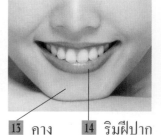

13 คาง
khaang
chin

14 ริมฝีปาก
rim-fǐi-pàak
lips

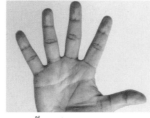

15 นิ้วมือ
níw mueh
fingers

16 นิ้วเท้า
níw tháo
toes

---

50 ส่วนต่างๆ ของร่างกายคุณมีอะไรบ้าง
Sùan tàang tàang khǎwng râang-gaay khun mii à-rai bâang?
How many parts of your body can you name?

51 คุณดูแลร่างกายของคุณยังไง
Khun duu-laeh râang-gaay khǎwng khun yang-ngai?
How do you take care of your body?

52 สูบบุหรี่ไม่ดีกับสุขภาพ
Sùup bù-rìi mâi-dii kàp sùk-khà-phâap.
Smoking is bad for your health.

53 ระวังอย่ากินและดื่มมากเกินไป
Rá-wang yàa gin láe dùehm mâak gerrn pai.
Be careful not to eat and drink too much.

54 อย่ากินของหวานกับขนมมากเกินไป
Yàa gin khǎwng wǎan gàp khà-nǒm mâak gerrn pai.
Don't eat too many sweets and snacks.

55 เพื่อสุขภาพแข็งแรง คุณควรออกกำลังกายทุกวัน
Phûea sùk-khà-phâap khǎeng-raehng khun khuan àwk-gam-lang-gaay thúk wan.
To stay healthy, you should exercise every day.

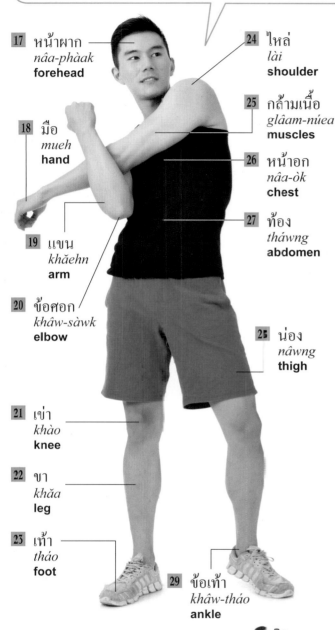

17 หน้าผาก
nâa-phàak
forehead

18 มือ
mueh
hand

19 แขน
khǎehn
arm

20 ข้อศอก
khâw-sàwk
elbow

21 เข่า
khào
knee

22 ขา
khǎa
leg

23 เท้า
tháo
foot

24 ไหล่
lài
shoulder

25 กล้ามเนื้อ
glâam-núea
muscles

26 หน้าอก
nâa-òk
chest

27 ท้อง
tháwng
abdomen

28 น่อง
nâwng
thigh

29 ข้อเท้า
khâw-tháo
ankle

Additional Vocabulary

36 อวัยวะ
à-wai-yá-wá
organs

37 ระบบย่อยอาหาร
rá-bòp yôy aa-hǎan
digestive system

38 ระบบหายใจ
rá-bòp hǎay-jai
respiratory system

39 ระบบประสาท
rá-bòp prà-sàat
nervous system

40 ระบบโครงกระดูก
rá-bòp khrohng grà-dùuk
skeletal system

41 ผิวหนัง
phǐw nǎng
skin

42 เลือด
lûeat
blood

43 หลอดเลือด
làwt lûeat
vessels

44 กระดูก
grà-dùuk
bone

45 หลอดเลือดแดง
làwt lûeat daehng
artery

46 หลอดเลือดดำ
làwt lûeat dam
vein

47 สุขภาพ
sùk-khà-phâap
health

48 ไม่สบาย
mâi sà-baay
illness

49 ท้อง
tháwng
stomach

30 สมอง
sà-mǎwng
brain

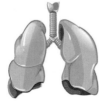

31 ปอด
pàwt
lungs

32 หัวใจ
hǔa-jai
heart

33 ไต
tai
kidneys

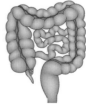

34 ลำไส้
lam-sâi
intestines

35 ตับ
tàp
liver

5 การนับเลขและตัวเลข

Gaan-náp lêhk láe tua-lêhk

Counting and numbers

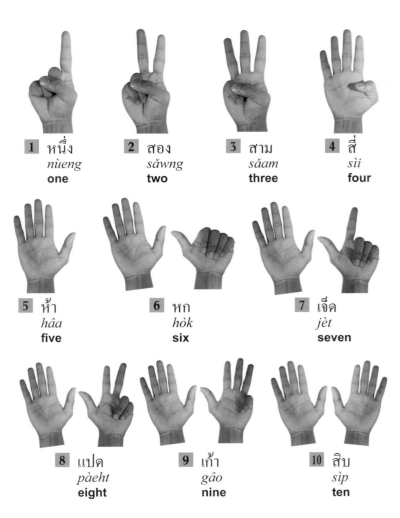

1 หนึ่ง *nùeng* one	**2** สอง *săwng* two	**3** สาม *săam* three	**4** สี่ *sìi* four
5 ห้า *hâa* five	**6** หก *hòk* six	**7** เจ็ด *jèt* seven	
8 แปด *pàeht* eight	**9** เก้า *gâo* nine	**10** สิบ *sìp* ten	

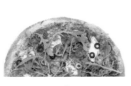

11 ครึ่ง *khrûeng* one half

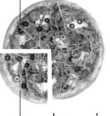

12 สามส่วนสี่ *săam sùan sìi* three quarters

13 หนึ่งส่วนสี่ *nùeng sùan sìi* one quarter

14 หนึ่งส่วนสาม *nùeng sùan săam* one third

15 สองส่วนสาม *săwng sùan săam* two thirds

จำนวนนับ *Jam-nuan náp*

Cardinal Numbers

0 ศูนย์ *sŭun* **zero**
11 สิบเอ็ด *sìp-èt* **eleven**
12 สิบสอง *sìp-săwng* **twelve**
13 สิบสาม *sìp-săam* **thirteen**
14 สิบสี่ *sìp-sìi* **fourteen**
15 สิบห้า *sìp-hâa* **fifteen**
16 สิบหก *sìp-hòk* **sixteen**
17 สิบเจ็ด *sìp-jèt* **seventeen**
18 สิบแปด *sìp-pàeht* **eighteen**
19 สิบเก้า *sìp-gâo* **nineteen**
20 ยี่สิบ *yîi-sìp* **twenty**
21 ยี่สิบเอ็ด *yîi-sìp-èt* **twenty-one**
22 ยี่สิบสอง *yîi-sìp-săwng* **twenty-two**
23 ยี่สิบสาม *yîi-sìp-săam* **twenty-three**
24 ยี่สิบสี่ *yîi-sìp-sìi* **twenty-four**
25 ยี่สิบห้า *yîi-sìp-hâa* **twenty-five**
26 ยี่สิบหก *yîi-sìp-hòk* **twenty-six**
27 ยี่สิบเจ็ด *yîi-sìp-jèt* **twenty-seven**
28 ยี่สิบแปด *yîi-sìp-pàeht* **twenty-eight**
29 ยี่สิบเก้า *yîi-sìp-gâo* **twenty-nine**
30 สามสิบ *săam-sìp* **thirty**
40 สี่สิบ *sìi-sìp* **forty**
50 ห้าสิบ *hâa-sìp* **fifty**
60 หกสิบ *hòk-sìp* **sixty**
70 เจ็ดสิบ *jèt-sìp* **seventy**
80 แปดสิบ *pàeht-sìp* **eighty**
90 เก้าสิบ *gâo-sìp* **ninety**
100 หนึ่งร้อย *nùeng-róy* **one hundred**
1,000 หนึ่งพัน *nùeng-phan* **one thousand**
10,000 หนึ่งหมื่น *nùeng-mùehn* **ten thousand**
100,000 หนึ่งแสน *nùeng-săehn* **one hundred thousand**
1,000,000 หนึ่งล้าน *nùeng-láan* **one million**
100,000,000 หนึ่งร้อยล้าน *nùeng-róy-láan* **one hundred million**
1,000,000,000 หนึ่งพันล้าน *nùeng-phan-láan* **one billion**
10,000,000,000 หนึ่งหมื่นล้าน *nùeng-mùehn-láan* **ten billion**

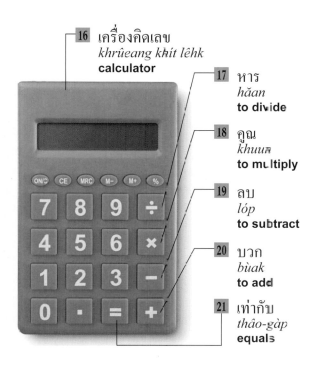

16 เครื่องคิดเลข
khrûeang khít lêhk
calculator

17 หาร
hǎan
to divide

18 คูณ
khuun
to multiply

19 ลบ
lóp
to subtract

20 บวก
bùak
to add

21 เท่ากับ
thâo-gàp
equals

เลขลำดับ *Lêhk lam-dàp* **Ordinal Numbers**
Note: To form an ordinal number, just add the word ที่ *'thîi'* in front of the number. For example:

1st ที่หนึ่ง *thîi nùeng* **first**
2nd ที่สอง *thîi sǎwng* **second**
3rd ที่สาม *thîi sǎam* **third**
4th ที่สี่ *thîi sìi* **fourth**
5th ที่ห้า *thîi hâa* **fifth**
6th ที่หก *thîi hòk* **sixth**
7th ที่เจ็ด *thîi jèt* **seventh**
8th ที่เปด *thîi pàeht* **eighth**
9th ที่เก้า *thîi gâo* **ninth**
10th ที่สิบ *thîi sìp* **tenth**
11th ที่สิบเอ็ด *thîi sìp-èt* **eleventh**
12th ที่สิบสอง *thîi sìp-sǎwng* **twelfth**
13th ที่สิบสาม *thîi sìp-sǎam* **thirteenth**
20th ที่ยี่สิบ *thîi yîi-sìp* **twentieth**
30th ที่สามสิบ *thîi sǎam-sìp* **thirtieth**
40th ที่สี่สิบ *thîi sìi-sìp* **fortieth**
50th ที่ห้าสิบ *thîi hâa-sìp* **fiftieth**
60th ที่หกสิบ *thîi hòk-sìp* **sixtieth**
70th ที่เจ็ดสิบ *thîi jèt-sìp* **seventieth**
80th ที่เปดสิบ *thîi pàeht-sìp* **eightieth**
90th ที่เก้าสิบ *thîi gâo-sìp* **ninetieth**
100th ที่หนึ่งร้อย *thîi nùeng-róy* **one-hundredth**
1,000th ที่หนึ่งพัน *thîi nùeng-phan* **one-thousandth**

Additional Vocabulary

22 ทั้งสอง
tháng sǎwng
two; both

23 เปอร์เซ็นต์
perr-sen
percent (%)

24 เศษส่วน
sèht sùan
fraction

25 เลขคู่
lêhk khûu
even numbers

26 เลขคี่
lêhk khîi
odd numbers

27 นับ
náp
to count

28 จำนวน
jam-nuan
numbers

29 ตัวเลข
tua-lêhk
digits

30 สองบวกสี่เท่ากับหก
Sǎwng bùak sìi thâo-gàp hòk.
Two plus four equals six.

31 สิบเอ็ดลบห้าเท่ากับหก
Sìp-èt lóp hâa thâo-gàp hòk.
Eleven minus five equals six.

32 สิบคูณสิบสองเท่ากับหนึ่งร้อยยี่สิบ
Sìp khuun sìp-sǎwng thâo-gàp nùeng-róy yîi-sìp.
Ten times twelve equals one hundred and twenty.

33 สี่สิบสองหารด้วยแปดเท่ากับห้าเศษหนึ่งส่วนสี่
Sìi-sìp-sǎwng hǎan dûay pàeht thâo-gàp hâa sèht nùeng sùan sìi.
Forty-two divided by eight equals five and a quarter.

6

ชีวิตประจำวัน
Chii-wít prà-jam-wan
Daily activities

5 ยืน
yeuhn
to stand

6 นั่ง
nâng
to sit

1 ร้องไห้
ráwng-hâi
to cry

2 หัวเราะ
hǔa-ráw
to laugh

3 ฟัง
fang
to listen

4 ดู; เห็น
duu; hěn
**to look;
see**

Additional Vocabulary

18 เสียง
sǐang
sound

19 ถาม
thǎam
to ask

20 เล่น
lêhn
to play

21 หายใจ
hǎay-jai
to breathe

22 ตอบ
tàwp
to answer

23 สังเกตเห็น
sǎng-gèht hěn
to catch sight of

24 ไปโรงเรียน
pai rohng-rian
go to school

25 โรงเรียนเลิก
rohng-rian lêrrk
school is over

26 ทำอาหาร;
เตรียมอาหาร
*tham aa-hǎan;
triam aa-hǎan*
**to cook; to prepare
a meal**

27 อาบน้ำ
àap-náam
to have a shower

28 สระผม
sà-phǒm
to wash my hair

29 พักผ่อน
phák-phàwn
to relax

30 กินอาหารเช้า
gin aa-hǎan cháo
to have breakfast

31 กินอาหารเที่ยง
gin aa-hǎan thîang
to have lunch

32 กินอาหารเย็น
gin aa-hǎan yen
to have dinner

33 เวลาว่าง
weh-laa wâang
leisure

34 ทำการบ้าน
tham gaan-bâan
study time

35 ทำงานบ้าน
tham ngaan-bâan
**to do household
chores**

36 วันธรรมดา
wan tham-má-daa
weekday

37 วันเสาร์อาทิตย์
wan sǎo-aa-thít
weekend

38 โกรธ
gròht
to get angry

39 แก้ปัญหา
gâeh pan-hǎa
to resolve

40 ขอ
khǎw
to request

41 เต็มใจ
tem-jai
**to be willing
(to do something)**

42 ตกลง
tòk-long
to agree

43 ไปทำงาน; เลิกงาน
*pai tham-ngaan;
lêrrk ngaan*
**go to work;
get off work**

44 ฉันต้องนอนแปดชั่วโมงทุกวัน
Chăn tâwng nawn pàeht chûa-mohng thúk wan.
I need eight hours of sleep every day.

7 นอน
nawn
to sleep

8 ดูทีวี
duu thii-wii
to watch TV

9 เขียน
khĭan
to write

10 ตื่นนอน
tùehn nawn
to wake up

11 แปรงฟัน
praehng fan
to brush teeth

12 คุย
khui
to talk

13 พูด
phûut
to speak

15 ย้าย
yâay
to move

16 ช่วย
chûay
to help

14 ทุกคนกินอาหารด้วยกัน
Thúk khon gin aa-hăan dûay gan.
Everybody eats together.

17 จูงหมา
juung măa
to walk the dog

45 วันธรรมดาตอนเย็นคุณทำอะไร
Wan tham-má-daa tawn-yen khun tham à-rai?
What do you do on weekday evenings?

46 วันเสาร์อาทิตย์คุณทำอะไร
Wan săo-aa-thít khun tham à-rai?
What do you do on weekends?

47 ทุกวันตอนเช้าคุณทำอะไรก่อน
Thúk wan tawn-cháo khun tham à-rai gàwn?
What is the first thing you do every morning?

48 ฉัน/ผมอาบน้ำกับแปรงฟัน
Chăn/Phŏm àap-náam gàp praehng-fan.
I take a shower and brush my teeth.

7 สี รูปร่าง และขนาด
Sĭi rûup-râang láe khà-nàat
Colors, shapes and sizes

1 สี
sĭi
colors

2 สีแดง
sĭi daehng
red

3 สีขาว
sĭi khăaw
white

4 สีดำ
sĭi dam
black

5 สีเหลือง
sĭi lŭeang
yellow

6 สีฟ้า
sĭi fáa
blue

7 สีเขียว
sĭi khĭaw
green

8 สีม่วง
sĭi mûang
purple

9 สีน้ำตาล
sĭi nám-taan
brown

10 สีเทา
sĭi thao
grey

11 สีส้ม
sĭi sôm
orange

12 สีชมพู
sĭi chom-phuu
pink

13 สีทอง
sĭi thawng
gold

14 สีเงิน
sĭi ngerrn
silver

15 สีเข้ม
sĭi khêhm
dark color

16 สีอ่อน
sĭi àwn
light color

44 คุณชอบสีอะไร
Khun châwp sĭi à-rai?
What is your favorite color?

45 ฉัน/ผมชอบสีแดง
Chăn/Phŏm châwp sĭi daehng.
My favorite color is red.

17 รุ้ง
rúng
a rainbow

22

18 สี่เหลี่ยมผืนผ้า
sìi-lìam phǔehn-phâa
a rectangle

19 หกเหลี่ยม
hòk lìam
a hexagon

20 แปดเหลี่ยม
pàeht lìam
an octagon

21 ห้าเหลี่ยม
hâa lìam
a pentagon

22 สี่เหลี่ยมจัตุรัส
sìi-lìam jà-tù-ràt
a square

23 หัวใจ
hǔa-jai
a heart

24 วงรี
wong-rii
an oval

25 ดาว
daaw
a star

26 สามเหลี่ยม
sǎam lìam
a triangle

27 วงกลม
wong-glom
a circle

28 สี่เหลี่ยมขนมเปียกปูน
sìi-lìam khà-nǒm piak-puun
a diamond

29 ไซส์เสื้อผ้า
sái sûea-phâa
clothing size

30 ไซส์เอ็ม
sái M
M size

31 ไซส์เอส
sái S
S size

32 ไซส์เอ็กซ์เอส
sái XS
XS size

33 ไซส์แอล
sái L
L size

34 ไซส์เอ็กซ์แอล
sái XL
XL size

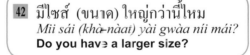

35 ใหญ่
yài
large

36 กลาง
glaang
medium

37 เล็ก
lék
small

42 มีไซส์ (ขนาด) ใหญ่กว่านี้ไหม
Mii sái (khà-nàat) yài gwàa níi mái?
Do you have a larger size?

43 แบบนี้มีสีอื่นไหม
Bàehp níi mii sǐi ùehn mái?
Do you have this in other colors?

Additional Vocabulary

38 รูปทรง
rûup song
shape

39 ไซส์; ขนาด
sái; khà-nàat
size

40 ใหญ่กว่า
yài gwàa
larger

41 เล็กกว่า
lék gwàa
smaller

คำตรงข้าม

Kham trong-khâam

8 | Opposites

1 ขึ้น ⬌ ลง
khûen ⬌ *long*
up ⬌ **down**

2 รับ ⬌ ให้
ráp ⬌ *hâi*
receive ⬌ **give**

3 มากกว่า ⬌ น้อยกว่า
mâak gwàa ⬌ *nóy gwàa*
more ⬌ **less**

6 ออก ⬌ เข้า
àwk ⬌ *khâo*
exit ⬌ **enter**

4 เก่า ⬌ ใหม่
gào ⬌ *mài*
old ⬌ **new**

5 สูง ⬌ เตี้ย
sǔung ⬌ *tîa*
tall ⬌ **short**

7 ดี ⬌ ไม่ดี
dii ⬌ *mâi dii*
good ⬌ **bad**

8 ยุ่ง ⬌ ว่าง
yûng ⬌ *wâang*
busy ⬌ **idle**

9 ยาว ⬌ สั้น
yaaw ⬌ *sân*
long ⬌ **short**

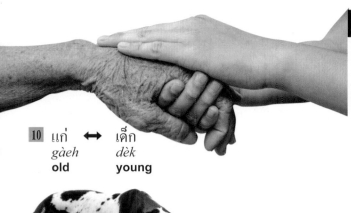

10 แก่ ⟷ เด็ก
gàeh — *dèk*
old — **young**

11 ใหญ่ ⟷ เล็ก
yài — *lék*
big — **small**

12 เปิด ⟷ ปิด
pèrrt — *pìt*
open — **closed**

13 อ้วน ⟷ ผอม
oûan — *phǎwm*
fat — **skinny**

14 ใส่ ⟷ ถอด
sài — *thàwt*
put on — **take off**

15 ยาก ⟷ ง่าย
yâak — *ngâay*
difficult — **easy**

16 มี ⟷ ไม่มี
mii — *mâi mii*
have — **do not have**

17 มา ⟷ ไป
maa — *pai*
come — **go**

18 ใช่ ⟷ ไม่ใช่
châi — *mâi châi*
yes — **no**

19 อิ่ม ⟷ หิว
ìm — *hǐw*
(eat till) full — **hungry**

20 ถึง ⟷ ออก
thǔeng — *àwk*
arrive — **depart**

21 อดีต ⟷ อนาคต
à-dìit — *à-naa-khót*
past — **future**

22 ข้างใน ⟷ ข้างนอก
khâang nai — *khâang nâwk*
inside — **outside**

23 ลืมแล้ว ⟷ จำได้
luehm láew — *jam dâi*
forgotten — **remembered**

24 เริ่ม ⟷ จบ
rêrrm — *jòp*
begin — **end**

25 ใกล้ ⟷ ไกล
glâi — *glai*
near — **far**

26 ผิด ⟷ ถูก
phìt — *thùuk*
wrong — **right**

27 จริง ⟷ ปลอม
jing — *plawm*
real — **fake**

28 เร็ว ⟷ ช้า
rew — *cháa*
fast — **slow**

29 สูง ⟷ ต่ำ
sǔung — *tàm*
high — **low**

30 ยืม ⟷ คืน
yuehm — *khuehn*
borrow — **return**

31 เสียใจ ⟷ ดีใจ
sǐa-jai — *dii-jai*
sad — **happy**

32 ดีใจตรงข้ามกับเสียใจ.
Dii-jai trong-khâam gàp sǐa-jai.
The opposite of happy is sad.

33 เย็นกับร้อนเป็นคู่ตรงข้ามกัน
Yen gàp ráwn pen khûu trong-khâam gan.
Cold and hot is also a pair of opposites.

34 คำตรงข้ามเป็นคำที่มีความหมายตรงข้ามกัน
Kham trong-khâam pen kham thîi mii khwaam-mǎay trong-khâam gan.
An antonym is a pair of words with opposite meanings.

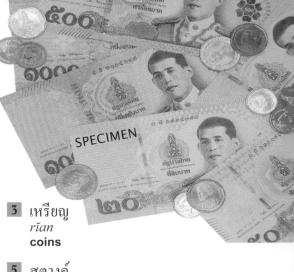

9 เงิน

Ngerrn

Talking about money

1 บาท
bàat; Baht
the official currency of Thailand; banknote; coin

2 ธนบัตร; แบงค์
thá-ná-bàt (formal); báehng (informal)
paper currency

4 ยี่สิบห้าสตางค์
yîi-sìp hâa sà-taang
25 satang

3 เหรียญ
rĭan
coins

5 สตางค์
sà-taang
satang (coin)

6 ห้าบาท
hâa bàat
5 baht

7 ห้าสิบสตางค์
hâa-sìp sà-taang
50 satang

10 หนึ่งบาท
nùeng bàat
1 baht

11 หนึ่งพันบาท
nùeng phan bàat
1000 baht

8 ยี่สิบบาท
yîi-sìp bàat
20 baht

12 สองบาท
săwng bàat
2 baht

13 ห้าสิบบาท
hâa-sìp bàat
50 baht

9 หนึ่งร้อยบาท
nùeng róy bàat
100 baht

14 สิบบาท
sìp bàat
10 baht

15 ห้าร้อยบาท
hâa róy bàat
500 baht

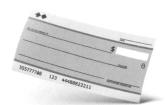

16 เช็ค
chék
check

17 เงินย่อย
ngerrn yôy
small change

18 บัตรเครดิต
bàt khreh-dìt
credit card

19 เงินเก็บ
ngerrn gèp
savings

20 อัตราแลกเงิน
àt-traa láehk ngerrn
currency exchange

21 ถอนเงิน
thǎwn ngerrn
to withdraw money

22 เหรียญ; เงิน
rǐan; ngerrn
coin; money

23 ราคา
raa-khaa
price

24 ลด
lót
discount

25 ถูก
thùuk
cheap

26 แพง
phaehng
expensive

27 ดอกเบี้ย
dàwk-bîa
interest

28 เงินกู้; เครดิต
ngerrn gûu; khreh-dìt
loan; credit

29 หนี้
nîi
debt

30 เงินฝาก
ngerrn fàak
bank deposit

31 เลขบัญชี
lêhk ban-chii
account number

32 ใบเสร็จ
bai-sèt
receipt

33 ค่างวด
khâa-ngûat
installment (payment)

34 ภาษี
phaa-sǐi
tax

35 เงินสด
ngerrn-sòt
cash

36 ราคาเท่าไรคะ
Raa-khaa thâo-rài khá?
How much does this cost?

37 สองร้อยห้าสิบบาทค่ะ
Sǎwng-róy hâa-sìp bàat khâ.
Two hundred and fifty baht (THB ฿ 250).

38 ลดได้ไหมคะ
Lót dâi-mái khá?
Can you give a discount?

39 โอเคค่ะ ลดได้ 50 บาท ค่ะ
Oh-kheh khá lót dâi hâa-sìp bàat khâ.
OK, 50 baht discount.

10 ไปช้อปปิ้ง
Pai cháwp-pîng
Going shopping

1 ซื้อ
súeh
to buy

43 เท่าไรคะ
Thâo-rài khá?
How much is it?

2 ขาย
khǎay
to sell

3 ซื้อของ
súeh khǎwng
to shop

4 ถุงช็อปปิ้ง
thǔng cháwp-pîng
shopping bag

5 นาฬิกา
naa-lí-gaa
watch

6 เสื้อผ้า
sûea-phâa
clothes

11 แว่นตา
wâehn-taa
**glasses;
spectacles**

14 เสื้อเชิ้ต
sûea-chérrt
shirt

7 เสื้อ
sûea
blouse

12 ถุงเท้า
thǔng-tháo
socks

15 เน็กไท
néhk-thai
necktie

9 กางเกงยีนส์
gaang-gehng yiin
jeans

8 กระโปรง
grà-prohng
skirt

10 กางเกงขายาว
gaang-gehng khǎa-yaaw
trousers

13 รองเท้า
rawng-tháo
shoes

16 หมวก
mùak
hat

Some useful shopping expressions:

46 ศูนย์การค้าใกล้ที่สุดอยู่ที่ไหน
Sǔun-gaan-kháa glâi thîi-sùt yùu thîi-nǎi?
Where is the nearest shopping center?

47 ลองได้ไหม
Lawng dâi-mái?
Can I try it on?

48 ห้องลองอยู่ที่ไหน
Hâwng-lawng yùu thîi-nǎi?
Where is the fitting room?

49 เอาอันนี้
Ao an-níi.
I'll take it.

50 รับบัตรเครดิตไหม
Ráp bàt khreh-dìt mái?
Do you accept credit cards?

51 ฉัน/ผมจะจ่ายเป็นเงินสด
Chǎn/Phǒm jà jàay pen ngerrn-sòt.
I'll pay in cash.

52 ขอใบเสร็จได้ไหม
Khǎw bai-sèt dâi-mái?
Could I have a receipt?

17 เครื่องสำอาง
khrûeang-sǎm-aang
cosmetics

18 ของเล่น
khǎwng-lêhn
toys

19 เข็มขัด
khěm-khàt
belt

20 ผ้าพันคอ
phâa phan-khaw
scarf

Additional Vocabulary

21 ลดราคา
lót raa-khaa
on sale

22 ร้าน
ráan
shop

23 ห้างสรรพสินค้า
hâang sàp-phá-sǐn-khâa
department store

24 บูติก
buu-tìk
boutique

25 พนักงานขาย
phá-nák-ngaan khǎay
shop staff

26 แคชเชียร์;
พนักงานเก็บเงิน
kháeht-chia;
phá-nák-ngaan gèp
ngerrn
cashier

27 ส่งถึงบ้าน
sòng thǔeng bâan
home delivery

28 เปรียบเทียบราคา
prìap-thîap raa-khaa
comparing prices

29 ซื้อของออนไลน์
súeh khǎwng awn-laay
online shopping

30 บัตรเครดิต
bàt khreh-dìt
credit card

31 เหมือนกับ
mǔean gàp
the same as

32 ทั้งหมด
tháng-mòt
altogether

33 แน่นอน
nâeh-nawn
certainly

34 โดยทั่วไป
dohy-thûa-pai
generally

35 มากกว่า; ยิ่งกว่า
mâak-gwàa;
yîng-gwàa
more; even more

36 ตัดสินใจ
tàt-sǐn-jai
decision

37 อื่น
ùehn
other

38 เอามา
ao-maa
to bring

39 สิ่งของ
sìng-khǎwng
things

40 บิล; ใบแจ้งราคา
bin; bai jâehng
raa-khaa
bill; invoice

41 ไม่เสียภาษี
mái sǐa phaa-sǐi
tax free

42 คืนเงิน
khuehn ngerrn
refund

44 มีภาษีไหม
Mii phaa-sǐi mái?
Is there any tax on this?

45 ขอคืนภาษีได้ไหม
Khǎw khuehn phaa-sǐi dâi-mái?
Can I refund the tax later?

ชีวิตในเมือง

11

Chii-wít nai mueang

Life in the city

1 โรงแรม
rohng-raehm
hotel

2 สนามบิน
sà-nǎam-bin
airport

3 ร้าน
ráan
shop

4 ถนน
thà-nǒn
street

5 ซูเปอร์มาร์เก็ต
súp-pêrr-maa-gét
supermarket

6 ปั๊มน้ำมัน
pám náam-man
**gas station;
petrol station**

7 ธนาคาร
thá-naa-khaan
bank

8 ศูนย์ประชุม
sǔun prà-chum
conference center

9 สถานีรถไฟ
sà-thǎa-nii rót-fai
train station

10 พิพิธภัณฑ์
phí-phít-thá-phan
museum

11 เมือง
mueang
city

12 ตึกสูง
tùek-sǔung
skyscraper

13 อพาร์ทเมนท์
à-pháat-mén
apartment

14 พิพิธภัณฑ์ศิลปะ
phi-phít-thá-phan sĭn-lá-pà
art museum

15 สนามกีฬา
sà-năam gii-laa
stadium

16 ไปรษณีย์
prai-sà-nii
post office

17 สถานีตำรวจ
sà-thăa-nii tam-rùat
police station

18 ทางด่วน
thaang-dùan
expressway

19 ยิม; ฟิตเนส
yim; fít-nèt
fitness gym

Additional Vocabulary

20 เกสต์เฮาส์
gèhs-háo
guesthouse

21 โรงหนัง
rohng-năng
cinema

22 ศูนย์การค้า; ห้าง
sŭun-gaan-kháa; hâang
shopping center; mall

23 ใจกลางเมือง
jai-glaang-mueang
downtown

24 ศูนย์กลางธุรกิจ
sŭun-glaang thú-rá-gìt
central business district (CBD)

25 นอกเมือง
nâwk-mueang
suburb

26 บ้าน
bâan
house

27 สะพาน
sà-phaan
bridge

28 ทางเดิน
thaang-derrn
sidewalk

29 เพื่อนบ้าน
phûean-bâan
neighbor

30 หัวมุมถนน
hŭa-mum thà-nŏn
street corner

31 อนุสาวรีย์
à-nú-săa-wá-rii
monument

32 โบสถ์
bòht
church

33 จราจร
jà-raa-jawn
traffic

34 คนเดินถนน
khon derrn thà-nŏn
pedestrian

35 ทางม้าลาย
thaang máa-laay
pedestrian crossing

36 วัด
wát
temple

---

39 คุณอยู่ในเมืองไหม หรืออยู่นอกเมือง
Khun yùu nai mueang măi? Rŭeh yùu nâwk mueang?
Do you live in the city? Or in the suburbs?

40 คุณไปทำงานยังไง
Khun pai tham-ngaan yang-ngai?
How do you go to work?

41 สนามบินไกลจากใจกลางเมืองแค่ไหน
Sà-năam-bin glai jàak jai glaang mueang khâeh năi?
How far is the airport from the city center?

42 คุณสุดาอยากอยู่ในเมือง
Khun Suda yàak yùu nai mueang.
Miss Suda wants to live in the city.

37 ไฟจราจร
fai jà-raa-jawn
traffic lights

38 ถนน
thà-nŏn
road

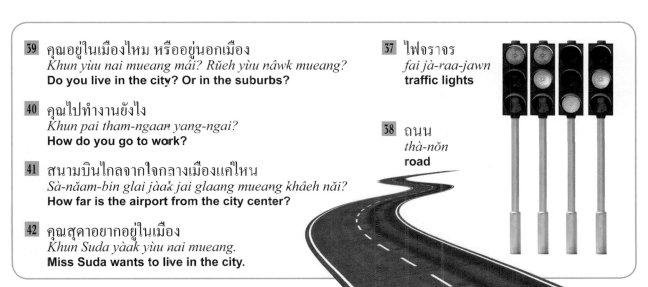

12

การเดินทาง
Gaan derrn-thaang
Getting around

1 รถยนต์
rót-yon
car

2 แท็กซี่
tháak-sîi
taxi

3 คนขับ
khon khàp
driver

4 เครื่องบิน
khrûeang bin
airplane

5 รถบรรทุก
rót ban-thúk
truck

6 รถขนขยะ
rót khŏn khà-yà
garbage truck

7 รถตู้ส่งของ
rót-tûu sòng khăwng
delivery van

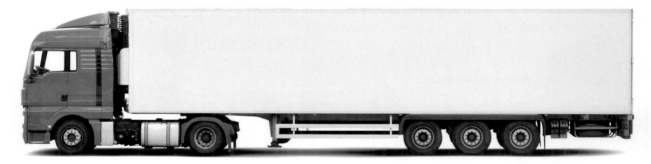

8 รถไฟความเร็วสูง
rót-fai khwaam-rew sŭung
high speed train

9 รถมอเตอร์ไซค์
rót maw-terr-sai
motorcycle

10 รถสปอร์ต
rót sà-pàwt
sports car

13 ป้ายรถเมล์
pâay rót-meh
bus stop

11 รถไฟใต้ดิน
rót-fai tâi-din
subway

12 รถเมล์
rót-meh
public bus

14 เรือ
ruea
ship; boat

15 รถไฟ
rót-fai
train

16 รถดับเพลิง
rót dàp-phlerrng
fire engine

17 รถราง
rót-raang
tram

18 รถสามล้อ
rót sǎam-láw
pedicab; trishaw

Additional Vocabulary

19 ผู้โดยสาร
phûu-dohy-sǎan
passenger

20 นั่งรถเมล์
nâng rót-meh
take a bus; by bus

21 ขึ้นรถเมล์
khûen rót-meh
catch a bus

22 ขึ้นรถไฟ
khûen rót-fai
catch a train

23 นั่งรถไฟ
nâng rót-fai
ride a train

24 ขับรถ
khàp rót
drive a car

25 ขี่จักรยาน
khìi jàk-grà-yaan
ride a bike

26 ช้าลง
châa long
slow down

27 ไปเร็วๆ
pai rew rew
go faster

28 เลี้ยวซ้าย/เลี้ยวขวา
lîaw sáay/lîaw khwǎa
turn left/turn right

29 ตรงไป
trong pai
go straight

30 ตารางรถไฟ
taa-raang rót-fai
train schedule

31 ช่องขายตั๋ว
châwng khǎay tǔa
ticket counter

32 เส้นทางรถเมล์
sêhn-thaang rót-meh
bus route

33 รถม้า
rót-máa
horse carriage

34 เรียกแท็กซี่
rîak tháek-sîi
to call a taxi

35 อูเบอร์
uu-bêrr
Uber

36 แกร๊บ
gráehp
Grab

37 จะเข้าเมืองไปรถอะไรดีที่สุด
Ja khâo-mueang pai rót à-rai dii thîi-sùt?
What is the best way to get downtown?

38 ไปรถเมล์ แท็กซี่ หรือขึ้นรถไฟใต้ดิน
Pai rót-meh tháek-sîi rǔeh khûen rót-fai tâi-din.
By bus, by taxi or take the subway.

39 สถานีรถไฟใต้ดินไปยังไง
Sà-thǎa-nii rót-fai tâi-din pai yang-ngai?
How do I get to the subway station?

13

ถามและบอกทาง
Thăam láe bàwk-thaang
Asking and giving directions

1 ที่ไหน
thîi-năi?
where?

6 ทิศเหนือ
thít nŭea
north

7 ทิศตะวันตกเฉียงเหนือ
thít tà-wan-tòk chĭang nŭea
northwest

8 ทิศตะวันออกเฉียงเหนือ
thít tà-wan-àwk chĭang nŭea
northeast

9 ทิศตะวันตก
thít tà-wan-tòk
west

10 ทิศตะวันออก
thít tà-wan-àwk
east

11 ทิศตะวันตกเฉียงใต้
thít tà-wan-tòk chĭang tâi
southwest

12 ทิศตะวันออกเฉียงใต้
thít tà-wan-àwk chĭang tâi
southeast

13 ทิศใต้
thít tâi
south

2 ที่นี่
thîi-nîi
here

14 ข้างหน้า
khâang-nâa
in front

15 ข้างหลัง
khâang-lăng
behind

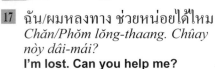

3 ที่นั่น
thîi-nân
there

Some common phrases for asking and giving directions:

16 ถามทาง
thăam thaang
asking directions

21 บอกทาง
bàwk thaang
giving directions

17 ฉัน/ผมหลงทาง ช่วยหน่อยได้ไหม
Chăn/Phŏm lŏng-thaang. Chûay nòy dâi-mái?
I'm lost. Can you help me?

22 ขอโทษค่ะ/ครับ ฉัน/ผมไม่รู้
Khăw-thôht khâ/khráp, chăn/phŏm mâi rúu.
I'm sorry, I don't know.

18 ทางนี้ไป...ใช่ไหม
Thaang níi pai ..... chai-mái?
Is this the way to … ?

23 ไปทางนี้
Pai thaang-níi.
It's this way.

24 ไปทางนั้น
Pai thaang-nán
It's that way.

19 ไกลแค่ไหน
Glai khâeh năi?
How far is it?

25 อยู่ทางซ้าย/ทางขวา
Yùu thaang-sáay/thaang-khwăa.
It's on the left/right.

20 ช่วยบอกได้ไหมอยู่ตรงไหนในแผนที่
Chûay bàwk dâi-mái yùu trong năi nai phăehn-thîi?
Can you show me on the map?

26 อยู่ติดกับ ...
Yùu tìt gàp ...
It's next to …

4 ข้างบน
khâang-bon
above

5 ข้างล่าง
khâang-lâang
below

28 ตรงกลาง
trong-glaang
middle; center

27 ข้างขวา
khâang-khwǎa
right side

29 ข้างซ้าย
khâang-sáay
left side

30 เลี้ยวซ้าย
líaw sáay
turn left

31 ตรงไป
trong pai
go straight

32 เลี้ยวขวา
líaw khwǎa
turn right

34 ข้างใน
khâang-nai
inside

33 ข้างนอก
khâang-nâwk
outside

Additional Vocabulary

35 หลงทาง
lǒng thaang
to be lost

36 ทาง
thaang
direction

37 ระยะทาง
rá-yá-thaang
distance

38 กิโลเมตร
gì-loh-méht
kilometer

39 ไมล์
mai
mile

40 เมตร
méht
meter

41 ฟุต
fút
foot

42 ใกล้
glâi
near

43 ไกล
glai
far

44 ตรงข้าม
trong-khâam
opposite

45 ตะวันออก
tà-wan-àwk
the East

46 ใต้
tâi
the South

47 ตะวันตก
tà-wan-tòk
the West

48 เหนือ
nǔea
the North

49 ข้าง
khâang
side

50 ใกล้ๆ
glâi glâi
nearby

51 สถานที่
sà-thǎan-thîi
place

52 ข้างหนึ่ง
khâang nùeng
one side

53 บอก
bàwk
to tell

54 ผ่าน
phàan
to go through

55 ออก
àwk
to leave

56 นานเท่าไร
naan thâo-rài
how much longer?

57 เดี๋ยวนี้
dǐaw-níi
immediately

58 ยอมให้
yawm-hâi
to allow

59 แล้ว
láehw
already

60 คิด
khít
to think

61 พิจารณา
phí-jaa-rá-naa
to consider

62 ช่วย
chûay
to help

63 กังวลใจ
gang-won jai
to feel anxious

อากาศ
14 | Aa-gàat
Talking about the weather

1 ร่ม
rôm
umbrella

2 เสื้อกันฝน
sûea gan-fǒn
raincoat

3 รองเท้าบู๊ท
rawng-tháo búut
boots

4 (ท้องฟ้า) สดใส
(tháwng-fáh) sòt-sǎi
clear (sky)

5 ฟ้าใส
fáa sǎi
clear day

6 มืดครึ้ม
mûeht khrúem
overcast

7 เมฆมาก
mêhk mâak
cloudy day

8 ลม
lom
wind

9 ลมแรง
lom raehng
windy

10 ฝน
fǒn
rain

11 ฝนตก
fǒn tòk
raining

12 ฟ้าผ่า
fáa-phàa
lightning

13 ฟ้าร้อง
fáa-ráwng
thunder

14 พายุฤดูร้อน
phaa-yú rúe-duu ráwn
thunderstorm

15 หิมะ
hì-má
snow

16 หิมะตก
hì-má tòk
to snow

17 พายุไต้ฝุ่น
phaa-yú tâi-fùn
typhoon

39 วันนี้อากาศดี พรุ่งนี้ฝนจะตก
Wan-níi aa-gàat dii. Phrûng-níi fǒn jà tòk.
It's a beautiful day today. Tomorrow will be rainy.

40 วันนี้ร้อนมาก พรุ่งนี้จะเย็นขึ้น
Wan-níi ráwn mâak. Phrûng-níi jà yen khûen.
It is too hot today. Tomorrow will be cooler.

18 เสื้อโค้ท; เสื้อแจ๊คเก็ต
sûea khóht; sûea jǽek-gêt
coat or jacket

19 เสื้อไหมพรม
sûea măi-phrom
sweater

Additional Vocabulary

32 อากาศ
aa-gàat
weather

33 พยากรณ์อากาศ
phá-yaa-gawn aa-gàat
weather forecast

34 อากาศดี
aa-gàat dii
good weather

35 อากาศไม่ดี
aa-gàat mâi-dii
bad weather

36 แดดร้อน
dàeht ráwn
sunny weather

37 มลพิษทางอากาศ
mon-lá-phít thaang-aa-gàat
air pollution

58 พายุเฮอร์ริเคน
phaa-yú herr-rí-khehn
hurricane

20 ร้อน
ráwn
hot

21 อากาศร้อน
aa-gàat ráwn
hot weather

22 หนาว
năaw
cold

23 อากาศหนาว
aa-gàat năaw
cold weather

24 เมฆ
mêhk
cloud

25 หมอก
màwk
fog

26 พระอาทิตย์
phrá-aa-thít
sun

27 พระจันทร์
phrá-jan
moon

28 พายุฝน
phaa-yú fŏn
rainstorm

29 ลูกเห็บ
lûuk-hèp
hail

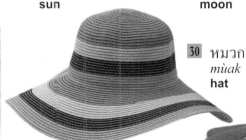

30 หมวก
mùak
hat

51 ถุงมือ
thŭng-mueh
gloves

37

บอกเวลา
Bàwk weh-laa
15 | **Telling time**

1 ชั่วโมง
chûa-mohng
hour

2 นาที
naa-thii
minute

3 วินาที
wí-naa-thii
second

6 นาฬิกา
naa-lí-gaa
clock

4 หกโมงเช้า; หกโมงเย็น
hòk mohng-cháo (morning);
hòk mohng-yen (evening)
6 o'clock

5 หกโมงห้านาที
hòk mohng hâa naa-thii
five minutes past six

8 หกโมงสิบห้านาที
hòk mohng sìp-hâa naa-thii
fifteen minutes past six

9 หกโมงครึ่ง
hòk mohng khrûeng
half past six

7 สิบห้านาที
sìp-hâa naa-thii
quarter (hour)

37 กี่โมง; กี่ทุ่ม
Gìi mohng (daytime)?
Gìi thûm (nighttime)?
What's the time?

38 แปดโมงครึ่ง; สองทุ่มครึ่ง
Pàeht mohng khrûeng (8.30 am);
Săwng thûm khrûeng (8.30 pm).
Half past eight.

10 หกโมงสี่สิบห้านาที
hòk mohng sìi-sìp-hâa
naa-thii
fifteen minutes to seven

11 หกโมงห้าสิบห้านาที
hòk mohng hâa-sìp-
hâa naa-thii
five minutes to seven

39 ขอโทษค่ะ ฉันมาสาย
Khăw-thôht khâ, chăn maa săay.
Sorry, I'm late.

40 ไม่เป็นไรครับ
Mâi-pen-rai khráp.
It's OK.

Additional Vocabulary

17 เวลา
weh-laa
time

18 เช้าตรู่
cháo-trùu
early morning

19 ตอนเช้า
tawn-cháo
in the morning; a.m.

20 เที่ยงวัน
thîang-wan
noon

21 ตอนบ่าย
tawn-bàay
in the afternoon; p.m.

22 เที่ยงคืน
thîang-khuehn
midnight

23 ตรงเวลา
trong weh-laa
punctual

24 เช้า
cháo
early

25 สาย
săay
late

25 ทีหลัง
thii-lăng
later

16 กลางคืน
glaang-khuehn
night

27 โมง; นาฬิกา
mohng; naa-lí-gaa (for official announcements)
o'clock

28 ก่อน
gàwn
before

29 ระหว่าง
rá-wàang
between; among

30 แป๊บเดียว; สักครู่
páep-diaw (informal); sàk-khrûu (formal)
a brief moment

31 เมื่อกี้นี้; เมื่อสักครู่
mûea-gîi níi (informal); mûea sàk-khrûu (formal)
a moment ago

32 แต่ก่อน
tàeh-gàwn
(in the) past

33 บ่อยๆ
bòy bòy
frequently

34 อีกแป๊บเดียว; อีกสักครู่
ìik páep-diaw (informal); ìik sàk-khrûu (formal)
in a moment

35 ทันที
than-thii
sudden

36 ในที่สุด
nai-thîi-sùt
finally

12 นาฬิกาปลุก
naa-lí-gaa plùk
alarm clock

13 นาฬิกาจับเวลา
naa-lí-gaa jàp-weh-laa
stopwatch

14 สมาร์ทวอทช์
sà-máat-wáwt
smartwatch

15 นาฬิกาข้อมือ
naa-lí-gaa khâw-mueh
wrist watch

41 เจอกันบ่ายสามโมงครับ
Jerr-gan bàay săam mohng!
See you at 3 p.m.!

16 ปีและวัน
Pii láe wan
Years and dates

1 ปฏิทิน
pà-tì-thin
calendar

2 ปี
pii
year

3 เดือน
duean
month

4 วัน
wan
day

SUNDAY	MONDAY	TUESDAY	WEDNESDAY	THURSDAY	FRIDAY	SATURDAY
New Year's Day 1	2	3	4	5	6	7
8	9	10	11	12	13	14
15	Martin Luther King Jr. Day 16	17	18	19	20	21
22	23	24	25	26	27	28
29	30	31				

9 วันอาทิตย์ *wan aa-thít* **Sunday**

10 วันจันทร์ *wan jan* **Monday**

11 วันอังคาร *wan ang-khaan* **Tuesday**

12 วันพุธ *wan-phút* **Wednesday**

13 วันพฤหัส *wan-phá-rúe-hàt* **Thursday**

14 วันศุกร์ *wan-sùk* **Friday**

15 วันเสาร์ *wan-săo* **Saturday**

5 วันอาทิตย์
wan aa-thít
Sunday

6 เมื่อวานนี้
mûea-waan-níi
yesterday

7 วันนี้
wan-níi
today

8 พรุ่งนี้
phrûng-níi
tomorrow

45 ฉันชอบเขียนไดอารี่
Chăn châwp khĭan dai-aa-rîi.
I like to keep a diary.

46 วันนี้วันศุกร์ที่ 27 มกราคม
Wan-níi wan-sùk thîi yìi-sìp-jèt mók-gà-raa-khom.
Today is Friday, January 27.

47 เมื่อวานนี้วันพฤหัสที่ 26 มกราคม
Mûea-waan-níi wan-phà-rúe-hàt thîi yìi-sìp-hòk mók-gà-raa-khom.
Yesterday was Thursday, January 26.

48 พรุ่งนี้จะเป็นวันเสาร์ที่ 28 มกราคม
Phrûng-níi jà pen wan-săo thîi yìi-sìp-pàeht mók-gà-raa-khom.
Tomorrow will be Saturday, January 28.

How to express years, months and dates in Thai:

In Thai, when reading the digits of the year, ปี *pii* (which means "year") comes first, then followed by the year.

2019 is ปีสองพันสิบเก้า *pii săwng-phan sìp-gâo*

2000 is ปีสองพัน *pii săwng-phan*

1994 is ปีหนึ่งพันเก้าร้อยเก้าสิบสี่ *pii nùeng-phan gâo-róy gâo-sìp-sìi*

2013 is ปีสองพันสิบสาม *pii săwng-phan sìp-săam*

The 12 months of the year in Thai are:

16 **January** มกราคม *mók-gà-raa-khom*

17 **February** กุมภาพันธ์ *gum-phaa-phan*

18 **March** มีนาคม *mii-naa-khom*

19 **April** เมษายน *meh-săa-yon*

20 **May** พฤษภาคม *phúet-sà-phaa-khom*

21 **June** มิถุนายน *mí-thù-naa-yon*

22 **July** กรกฎาคม *gà-rá-gà-daa-khom*

23 **August** สิงหาคม *sing-hăa-khom*

24 **September** กันยายน *gan-yaa-yon*

25 **October** ตุลาคม *tù-laa-khom*

26 **November** พฤศจิกายน *phrúet-sà-jì-gaa-yon*

27 **December** ธันวาคม *than-waa-khom*

Dates are expressed as วันที่ *wan-thîi* (which means "date") plus the date. For example:

February 5 วันที่ 5 กุมภาพันธ์ *wan-thîi hâa gum-phaa-phan*

March 31 วันที่ 31 มีนาคม *wan-thîi săam-sìp-èt mii-naa-khom*

April 1 วันที่ 1 เมษายน *wan-thîi nùeng meh-săa-yon*

July 4 วันที่ 4 กรกฎาคม *wan-thîi sìi gà-rá-gà-daa-khom*

December 25 วันที่ 25 ธันวาคม *wan-thîi yîi-sìp-hâa than-waa-khom*

49 คุณเกิดวันที่เท่าไร
Khun gèrrt wan-thîi thâo-rài?
When is your birthday?

50 ฉันเกิดวันที่ 31 มกราคม
Chăn gèrrt wan-thîi săam-sìp-èt mók-gà-raa-khom.
My birthday is on January 31.

Additional Vocabulary

28 ปีที่แล้ว
pii thîi-láehw
last year

29 ปีก่อน
pii gàwn
the year before

30 ปีนี้
pii níi
this year

31 ปีหน้า
pii náa
next year

32 ปีต่อไป
pii tàw-pai
the year after next

33 อาทิตย์; สัปดาห์
aa-thít (informal);
sàp-daa (formal)
week

34 ปี
pii
years (of age)

35 ปีอธิกสุรทิน
pii à-thí-gà-sù-rá-thin
leap year

36 วันที่
wan-thîi
day of a month

37 ทศวรรษ
thót-sà-wát
decade (10 years)

38 ศตวรรษ
sàt-tà-wát
century (100 years)

39 สหัสวรรษ
sà-hàt-sà-wát
millennium (1000 years)

40 อาทิตย์ที่แล้ว
aa-thít thîi-láehw
last week

41 เดือนที่แล้ว
duean thîi-láehw
last month

42 อาทิตย์หน้า
aa-thít náa
next week

43 เดือนหน้า
duean náa
next month

44 ไดอารี่
dai-aa-rîi
diary

ฤดูในหนึ่งปี
Rúe-duu nai nùeng pii
The seasons of the year

1 ฤดูใบไม้ผลิ
rúe-duu bai-mái-phlì
spring

2 ฤดูร้อน
rúe-duu ráwn
summer

3 ฤดูใบไม้ร่วง
rúe-duu bai-mái-rûang
autumn

4 ฤดูหนาว
rúe-duu năaw
winter

5 ฤดูฝน
rúe-duu fŏn
rainy

6 อุ่น
ùn
warm

7 ลมโชย
lom chohy
a gentle breeze

8 ดอกมะลิ
dàwk má-lí
jasmine blossoms

9 ออกดอก
àwk dàwk
to flower

10 ฝนตกปรอยๆ
fŏn-tòk proy proy
to drizzle

11 ที่บังแดด
thîi bang-dàeht
sun shade

12 เล่นน้ำ
lêhn náam
water play

13 ปั้นตุ๊กตาหิมะ
pân túk-gà-taa hì-má
to make a snowman

The changing colors of the seasons.

ดอกไม้บาน
dàwk-mái baan
spring blossoms

ใบไม้ผลิใบ
bai-mái phlì bai
summer greenery

ใบไม้เปลี่ยนสี
bai-mái plìan sĭi
autumn foliage

หิมะตก
hì-má tòk
winter snow

14 เกี่ยวข้าว
gìaw khâaw
to harvest

15 พัด
phát
fan

16 ปาก้อนหิมะ
paa gâwn hì-má
snowball fights

17 ครีมกันแดด
khriim gan dàeht
sunblock lotion

18 พืชผล
phûeht phŏn
crops

Additional Vocabulary

19 สี่ฤดู
sìi rúe-duu
four seasons

20 ก่อน
gàwn
former

21 ที่จริงแล้ว
thîi-jing-láew
actually

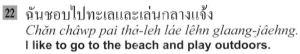

22 ฉันชอบไปทะเลและเล่นกลางแจ้ง
Chăn châwp pai thá-leh láe lêhn glaang-jâehng.
I like to go to the beach and play outdoors.

23 หนึ่งปีมีกี่ฤดู
Nùeng pii mii gìi rúe-duu?
How many seasons are there in a year?

24 หนึ่งปีมีสี่ฤดู
Nùeng pii mii sìi rúe-duu.
There are four seasons in a year.

25 คุณชอบฤดูไหนมากที่สุด
Khun châwp rúe-duu năi mâak thîi-sùt?
Which season do you like best?

26 ฉันชอบฤดูร้อน
Chăn châwp rúe-duu ráwn.
My favorite season is summer.

วันหยุดเทศกาล
Wan-yùt thêht-sà-gaan
Celebrating the holidays

1 เทศกาลวันหยุด
thêht-sà-gaan wan-yùt
festival; holiday

2 ปีใหม่
pii-mài
New Year

3 พลุ; ดอกไม้ไฟ
phlú; dàwk-mái fai
fireworks

4 วันปีใหม่
wan pii-mài
New Year's Day

5 วันสงกรานต์
wan sŏng-graan
**Water Festival;
Thai New Year**

6 วันตรุษจีน
wan trùt-jiin
Chinese New Year

7 วันลอยกระทง
wan loy-grà-thong
Lantern Festival

8 บุญบั้งไฟ
bun-bâng-fai
Rocket Festival

9 แห่เทียนพรรษา
hàeh thian phan-săa
Candle Festival

10 ผีตาโขน
phĭi-taa-khŏhn
Ghost Festival

11 เทศกาลกินเจ
thêht-sà-gaan gin-jeh
Vegetarian Festival

34 สวัสดีปีใหม่
Sà-wàt-dii pii-măi!
Happy New Year!

12 วันพ่อ
wan phâw
Father's Day

13 วันแม่
wan mâeh
Mother's Day

14 วันวาเลนไทน์
wan waa-len-taai
Valentine's Day

24 วันเกิด
wan gèrrt
birthday

25 ไปงานวันเกิด
pai ngaan wan-gèrrt
attend a birthday party

26 ปิดเทอม
pìt-therrm
school holidays

27 ครบรอบ
khróp-ráwp
anniversary

28 วันวิสาขบูชา
wan wí-săa-khà-bou-chaa
Visakha Puja Day (6th Thai lunar month)

29 วันอาสาฬหบูชา
wan aa-săn-hà-bou-chaa
Asalha Puja (8th Thai lunar month)

30 วันเข้าพรรษา
wan khâo-phan-săa
Buddhist Lent Day/ Beginning of Vassa (8th Thai lunar month)

31 สุขสันต์วันเกิด
Sùk-săn wan-gèrrt!
Happy birthday!

21 ของขวัญ
khwăwng-khwan
gift

15 ช็อคโกแลต
cháwk-goh-láet
chocolates

16 ดอกกุหลาบ
dàwk-gù-làap
roses

17 วันขอบคุณพระเจ้า
wan khàwp-khun phrá-jâo
Thanksgiving

18 วันฮาโลวีน
wan haa-loh-wiin
Halloween

32 สุขสันต์วันคริสต์มาส
Sùk-săn wan-khrís-mâat!
Merry Christmas!

22 คริสต์มาส
khrís-mâat
Christmas

23 ซานตาคลอส
saan-taa-khláwt
Santa Claus

19 วันอีสเตอร์
wan iis-têrr
Easter

20 วันเด็ก
wan dèk
Children's Day

33 มาเล่นสงกรานต์ด้วยกัน
Maa lêhn sŏng-graan dûay gan.
Please join us for the Thai New Year celebrations.

19

ฉัน/ผมชอบเรียน
Chăn/Phŏm châwp rian
I love to learn

1 สอบ
sàwp
exams

2 อ่านหนังสือ
àan năng-sŭeh
reading

3 เรียน
rian
to learn; to study

4 คณิตศาสตร์; เลข
khá-nít-sàat (formal);
lêhk (informal)
mathematics

5 พละ
phá-lá
physical education

6 ตอบ
tàwp
to answer

7 หนังสือ
năng-sŭeh
books

8 ข่าว
khàaw
the news

9 หนังสือพิมพ์
năng-sŭeh-phim
newspaper

10 นิตยสาร
nít-tà-yá-săan
magazine

11 จดหมาย
jòt-măay
letter

12 พจนานุกรม
phòt-jà-naa-nú-grom
dictionary

13 ปากกา
pàak-gaa
pen

14 ยางลบ
yang-lóp
eraser

15 ปากกาเคมี; ปากกามาร์คเกอร์
pàak-gaa kheh-mii; pàak-gaa máak-gêrr
marker pen

16 กบเหลาดินสอ
gàp lǎo din-sǎw
pencil sharpener

17 ไม้บรรทัด
mái ban-thát
ruler

18 สมุด
sà-mùt
notebook

19 ปากกาไฮไลท์
pàak-gaa hai-lái
highlighter

20 ดินสอ
din-sǎw
pencil

21 กรรไกร
gan-grai
scissors

Additional Vocabulary

22 ชั้น
chán
grade; class

23 เข้าใจ
khâo-jai
to understand

24 ฝึกฝน
fùek-fǒn
to practice

25 ทบทวน
thóp-thuan
to review

26 คำถาม
kham-thǎam
a question; problem

27 การบ้าน
gaan-bâan
homework

28 วรรณคดี
wan-ná-khá-dii
literature

29 ประวัติศาสตร์
prà-wàt-sàat
history

30 คำ
kham
word

31 เรื่อง
rûeang
story

32 การบ้าน
gaan-bâan
assignment

33 รัก; ชอบ
rák; châwp
love; like

34 เรขาคณิต
reh-khǎa-khá-nít
geometry

35 วิทยาศาสตร์
wít-thá-yaa-sàat
science

36 สังคมศึกษา
sǎng-khom sùek-sǎa
social studies

37 เศรษฐศาสตร์
sèht-thà-sàat
economics

38 พีชคณิต
phii-chá khá-nít
algebra

39 ฟิสิกส์
fí-sìk
physics

40 เคมี
kheh-mii
chemistry

41 ชีววิทยา
chii-wá wít-thá-yaa
biology

42 แคลคูลัส
khael-khuu-lát
calculus

43 ภูมิศาสตร์
phuum-mí-sàat
geography

44 สอบ
sàwp
test

45 ความสามารถ
khwaam-sǎa-mâat
talent; ability

46 จริงจัง
jing-jang
conscientious; serious

47 ระดับ
rá-dàp
level (of achievement)

48 ปรับปรุง
pràp-prung
to improve

49 สูงสุด
sǔung-sùt
top; extreme

50 เป้าหมาย
pâo-mǎay
purpose

51 ฉันชอบหนังสือ
Chǎn cháwp nǎng-sǔeh!
I love books!

52 คุณชอบวิชาอะไร
Khun cháwp wii-chaa à-rai?
What is your favorite subject?

53 ฉันชอบวรรณคดีกับประวัติศาสตร์
Chǎn/Phǒm cháwp wan-ná-khá-dii gàp prà-wàt-sàat.
I like literature and history.

โรงเรียน
Rohng-rian
At school

1 กระดานขาว
grà-daan khǎaw
whiteboard

2 กระดานดำ
grà-daan dam
blackboard

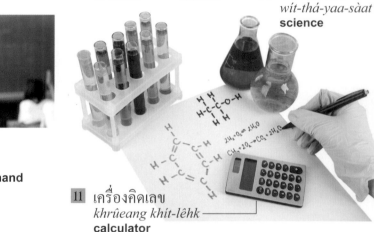

3 ห้องสมุด
hâwng sà-mùt
library

4 ห้องเรียน
hâwng rian
classroom

5 สอน
sǎwn
to teach

6 ครู
khruu
teacher

7 เครื่องถ่ายเอกสาร
khrûeang thàay-èhk-gà-sǎan
photocopier

9 ยกมือ
yók mueh
raise your hand

8 ถ่ายเอกสาร
thàay-èhk-gà-sǎan
to photocopy

10 อาจารย์
aa-jaan
professor; lecturer

12 วิทยาศาสตร์
wít-thá-yaa-sàat
science

11 เครื่องคิดเลข
khrûeang khít-lêhk
calculator

48 อยากให้ช่วยสอนการบ้านไหม
Yàak hâi chûay sǎwn gaan-bâan mái?
Do you need help with your assignment?

13 เพื่อนร่วมชั้น
phûean rûam chán
classmates

14 ห้องเรียน
hâwng rian
lecture hall

15 นักเรียน; นักศึกษา
nák-rian (school);
nák-sùek-sǎa (university)
student

16 โรงเรียน
rohng-rian
school

17 ครูใหญ่
khruu yài
principal

18 หอประชุม
hăw prà-chum
auditorium

19 ห้องคอมพิวเตอร์
hâwng khawm-phíw-têrr
computer lab

20 ห้องแล็บ
hâwng làep
laboratory

21 พยัญชนะ
phá-yan-chá-ná
alphabet

22 เกรด
grèht
grades

23 ฉลาด
chà-làat
intelligent; clever

24 เรียนภาคค่ำ
rian phâak-khâm
night class

25 หัวข้อ
hŭa-khâw
topic

26 เกิน
gerrn
to exceed

27 หนังสือเรียน
năng-sŭeh rian
textbook

28 หนังสือแบบฝึกหัด
năng-sŭeh bàehp-fùek-hàt
workbook

29 โรงเรียนเอกชน
rohng-rian èhk-gà-chon
private school

30 โรงเรียนรัฐบาล
rohng-rian rát-thà-baan
public school

31 โรงเรียนเตรียมอนุบาล
rohng-rian triam à-nú-baan
nursery school

32 เข้าเรียนชั้นประถม
khâo rian chán prà-thŏm
to attend elementary school

33 โรงเรียนประถมศึกษา
rohng-rian prà-thŏm sùek-săa
elementary school

34 โรงเรียนมัธยมศึกษาตอนต้น
rohng-rian mát-thá-yom sùek-săa tawn-tôn
middle school

35 โรงเรียนมัธยมศึกษาตอนปลาย
rohng-rian mát-thá-yom sùek-săa tawn-plaay
senior high school

36 มหาวิทยาลัย
má-hăa-wít-thá-yaa-lai
university; college

37 นักศึกษาปีหนึ่ง
nák-sùek-săa pii nùeng
freshman year in college

38 นักศึกษาปีสอง
nák-sùek-săa pii săwng
sophomore year in college

39 นักศึกษาปีสาม
nák-sùek-săa pii săam
junior year in college

40 นักศึกษาปีสี่
nák-sùek-săa pii sìi
senior year in college

41 วิชาเอก
wí-chăa èhk
to major

42 เรียนจบ; จบการศึกษา
rian jòp (informal); jòp gaan-sùek-săa (formal)
to graduate

43 คุณเรียนอยู่ปีอะไร
Khun rian yùu pii à-rai?
What year are you?

44 ฉัน/ผม เรียนมหาวิทยาลัยปีสอง
Chăn/Phŏm rian má-hăa-wít-thá-yaa-lai pii săwng.
I'm a sophomore in college.

45 ฉัน/ผม เรียนวิชาเอกคณิตศาสตร์
Chăn/Phŏm rian wí-chăa-èhk khá-nít-sàat.
I'm majoring in math.

46 คุณเรียนวิชาเอกอะไร
Khun rian wí-chăa-èhk à-rai?
What is your major?

47 คุณต้องเป็นคนฉลาดมาก
Khun tâwng pen khon chà-làat mâak!
You must be very smart!

21

เรียนภาษาไทย
Rian phaa-sǎa Thai
Learning Thai

1 พูดภาษาไทยไม่ยาก
Phuut phaa-sǎa thai mâi yâak.
Thai is not a difficult language to speak.

2 แต่ต้องใช้เวลาเรียนรู้ห้าเสียงวรรณยุกต์
Tàeh tâwng chái weh-laa rian rúu hâa sǐang wan-ná-yúk.
But it takes time to learn the five tones.

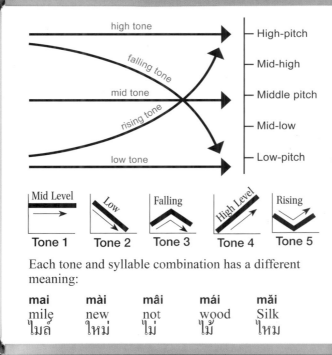

Each tone and syllable combination has a different meaning:

mai	mài	mâi	mái	mǎi
mile	new	not	wood	Silk
ไมล์	ใหม่	ไม่	ไม้	ไหม

3 และการเรียนตัวเขียนพยัญชนะยาก
Láe gaan rian tua khǐan phá-yan-chá-ná yâak.
And learning all the written characters is difficult.

4 ภาษาไทย
phaa-săa thai
Thai language

5 อักษรไทย
àk-săwn thai
Thai character

6 คำศัพท์
kham-sàp
vocabulary

7 วรรณยุกต์
wan-ná-yúk
tone (of a Thai character)

8 สำเนียง
săm-niang
accent

9 ความหมาย
khwaam-măay
meaning

10 สำนวน
săm-nuan
idiom

11 ประโยค
prà-yòhk
sentence

12 คำพูด
kham-phûut
phrase

13 คำ
kham
words

14 บทความย่อ
bòt-khwaam yâw
short essay

15 กลอน
glawn
poem

16 บทความ
bòt-khwaam
essay

17 วัฒนธรรม
wát-thá-ná-tham
culture

18 ไวยากรณ์
wai-yaa-gawn
grammar

19 การแปล
gaan-plaeh
translation

20 ภาษาศาสตร์
phaa-săa-sàat
linguistics

21 บทเรียน
bòt-rian
lesson

22 หลักสูตร
làk-sùut
course; academic program

23 การบ้าน
gaan-bâan
assignment

24 หนังสือแบบฝึกหัด
năng-sŭeh bàehp-fùek-hàt
exercise book

25 พื้นฐาน
phúehn-thăan
simple

26 เข้าใจ
khâo-jai
to understand

27 ง่าย
ngâay
easy

28 ยาก
yâak
difficult

29 ฝึก
fùek
to drill

30 พยายาม
phá-yaa-yaam
to strive

31 เตรียมตัว
triam-tua
to prepare

32 บัตรคำ
bàt kham
flashcards

33 การคัดลายมือ
gaan khát laay-mueh
calligraphy

35 พยัญชนะ
phá-yan-chá-ná
consonant

34 ตัวอักษร
tua àk-săwn
alphabet; letter

36 หัดเขียนตัวอักษรไทย
hàt khĭan tua àk-săwn Thai
practice writing Thai alphabets

37 พยัญชนะไทยมี 44 ตัว
Phá-yan-chá-ná Thai mii sìi-sìp- sìi tua.
There are 44 Thai consonants.

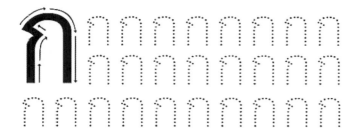

ลักษณนาม

Lák-sà-nà-naam

22 | Counting words

Also known as "measure words"

1 น้ำตาลสองซอง
náam-taan sǎwng sawng
two packets of sugar

2 หนังสือสามเล่ม
nǎng-sǔeh sǎam lêhm
three books

3 รองเท้าหนึ่งคู่
rawng-tháo nùeng khûu
one pair of shoes

4 ตั๋วห้าใบ
tǔa hâa bai
five tickets

5 เสื้อผ้าแปดชุด
sûea-phâa pàeht chút
eight pieces of clothing

6 แกงหนึ่งถ้วย
gaehng nùeng thûay
one bowl of soup

8 เก้าอี้หนึ่งตัว
gâo-îi nùeng tua
one chair

7 รถสามคัน
rót sǎam khan
three cars

Counting words or measure words are used to quantify things, just as in English when we say "three sheets of paper" or "two cups of coffee." In Thai, however, the number and classifier come after the noun = "noun + number + classifier", i.e., *grà-dàat săam phàaen* = "paper + three + sheets" (= three sheets of paper) or *gaa-faeh săam gâehw* = "coffee + two + cups" (= two cups of coffee.)

Some common measure words in Thai are listed below.

MEASURE WORDS	MAIN USES	Example
ห่อ *hàw*	Packets, packages, bundles	**9** คุ้กกี้หนึ่งห่อ *khúk-gîi nùeng hàw* **a packet of cookies**
เล่ม *lêhm*	Books, notebooks, magazines	**10** พจนานุกรมหนึ่งเล่ม *pót-jà-naa-nú-grom nùeng lêhm* **a dictionary**
คู่ *khûu*	Objects that come in pairs	**11** ถุงเท้าสองคู่ *thŭng-tháo săwng khûu* **two pairs of socks**
ตัว *tua*	Clothing, furniture, animal	**12** เสื้อสามตัว *sûea săam tua* **three shirts**
ใบ *bai*	Leaves, tickets, hollow objects (e.g., cups, bowls, hats. tin-cans, eggs, fruit, bags)	**13** หมวกสองใบ *mùak săwng bai* **two hats**
ถ้วย *thûay*	Food served in bowl (e.g., rice, soup, noodles, etc.)	**14** ข้าวหกถ้วย *khâaw hòk thûay* **six bowls of rice**
กลุ่ม *glùm*	Groups of people	**15** นักเรียนหนึ่งกลุ่ม *nák-rian nùeng glùm* **a group of students**
คน *khon*	General measure word for individual people	**16** พี่ชายสี่คน *phîi-chaay sìi khon* **four older brothers**
คัน *khan*	Vehicles (except trains), objects with handles	**17** จักรยานหลายคัน *jàk-grà-yaan lăay khan* **several bicycles**
ชั้น *chán*	Floor/story (as in a building), layer	**18** ชั้นห้า *chán-hâa* **the fifth floor**
ขวด *khùat*	Liquid (e.g., drinks/beverages) served in bottles	**19** น้ำหนึ่งขวด *náam nùeng khùat* **a bottle of water**
อัน *an*	General classifier for small objects (you can use it if you cannot remember the right classifier)	**20** แปรงสีฟันหนึ่งอัน *praehng-sĭi-fan nùeng an* **a toothbrush**
กิโลกรัม *gì-loh-gram*	kilogram (to express in weights)	**21** แอปเปิ้ล 1 กิโลกรัม *áep-pêrrn nùeng gì-loh-gram* **1 kg of apples**

คอมพิวเตอร์กับอินเทอร์เน็ต

23

Khawm-phíw-têrr gàp In-terr-nèt

Computers and the Internet

1 คอมพิวเตอร์
khawm-phíw-têrr
computers

2 หน้าจอ
nâa-jaw
screen

3 แท็บเล็ต
táep-lèt
tablet

6 แล็ปท็อป
làep-tháwp
laptop

7 เข้าถึงโลกออนไลน์ในประเทศไทยได้ง่าย
Khâo thŭeng lôhk awn-laai nai prà-thêht thai dâi ngâay.
It is easy to get online in Thailand.

4 คอมพิวเตอร์ตั้งโต๊ะ
khawm-phíw-têrr tâng tóh
desktop computer

5 แป้นพิมพ์; คีย์บอร์ด
pâehn phim; khii-bàwt
keyboard

8 วิดีโอเกม
wí-dii-oh gehm
video game

9 แผ่นรองเมาส์
phàehn rawng máo
mousepad

10 เม้าส์
máo
mouse

11 สแกน
sà-gaehn
to scan

12 ซีดี; ดีวีดี
sii-dii; dii-wii-dii
CD/DVD

13 แฟลชไดรฟ์
flàeht drái
USB flash drive

14 พอร์ต
phàwt
ports

15 อีเมล
ii-mehl
email

16 ลงชื่อเข้าใช้
long chûeh kháo chái
to sign in

17 รหัสผ่าน
rá-hàt phàan
password

18 เว็บไซต์
wép-sái
website

19 ซอฟต์แวร์
sáwp-waeh
software

20 ระบบปฏิบัติการ
rá-bòp pà-tì-bàt-gaan
operating system

21 ไวรัส
wai-rát
virus

22 ไฟล์
faay
file

23 เชื่อมต่อเครือข่าย
chûeam-tàw khruea-khàay
networking

24 หน้าเว็บ
nâa wép
web page

25 ออกแบบเว็บไซต์
àwk-bàep wép-sái
web design

26 ที่อยู่เว็บไซต์; ยูอาร์แอล
thîi-yùu wép-sái; yuu-aa-ael
web address/URL

27 แอปพลิเคชั่น
áep-phlí-kheh-chân
application (computer program)

28 เข้าอินเทอร์เน็ต
khâo in-terr-nèt
Internet access

29 คลิก
khlík
to click

30 ดาวน์โหลด
daaw-lòht
to download

31 เชื่อมต่อออนไลน์
chûeam-tàw awn-laai
to go online

32 ออนไลน์
awn-laai
online

33 ห้วงแชท
hûewng cháeht
chat room

34 การ์ดเครือข่าย
gcat khruea-khàay
network card

35 มัลติมีเดีย
man-tì-mii-dia
multimedia

36 บล็อก
blàwk
blog

37 เบราว์เซอร์
bráo-sêrr
browser

38 แชทออนไลน์
cháeht awn-laai
to chat online

39 ส่งอีเมล
sòng ii-mehl
to send email

40 ค้นหาออนไลน์
khôn-hăa awn-laai
online search

41 วายฟาย
waay-faay
wifi

42 เครือข่ายเคเบิล
khruea-khàay kheh-bêrrn
cable network

43 ตามที่
taam-thîi
according to

44 หลังจากนั้น
lăng-jàak-nán
after that

45 เพราะ
phráw
because

46 นอกจากนี้
nâwk-jàak-níi
in addition

47 พิเศษ
phí-sèt
extraordinary

48 ความปลอดภัยบนเครือข่าย
khwaam plòt-phai bon khruea-khàay
network security

49 งานอดิเรกของผมคือเล่นเกมออนไลน์
Ngaan à-dì-rèk khăwng phŏm khueh lêhn gehm awn-laai.
My hobby is online gaming.

50 มาแชทออนไลน์กัน
Maa cháet awn-laai gan.
Let's chat online.

51 คุณใช้แอพอะไร ฉัน/ผมใช้วีแชท
Khun châi áep à-rai? Chăn/phŏm chai Wii-cháet.
What app do you use? I use WeChat.

52 โอเค ฉัน/ผมจะส่งเอกสารให้คุณทางคอมพิวเตอร์
Oh-kheh Chăn/phŏm jà sòng èk-gà-săan hâi khun thaang khawm-phíw-têrr.
Okay, I'm now sending you the documents via computer.

24

ฉัน/ผมชอบสมาร์ทโฟน!
Chǎn/Phǒm châwp sà-máat-fohn!
I love my smartphone!

1 สมาร์ทโฟน
sà-máat-fohn
smartphone

2 เพื่อนออนไลน์
phûean awn-laai
online friends

3 ซื้อของออนไลน์
súeh-khǎwng awn-laai
online shopping

4 ร้านอินเตอร์เน็ต
ráan in-terr-nèt
internet cafes

5 ทวิตเตอร์
thá-wít-têrr
Twitter

6 วีแชท
wii-cháet
WeChat

7 โทรศัพท์แอนดรอยด์
thoh-rá-sàp aehn-droy
Android phones

8 โทรศัพท์แอปเปิล (ไอโฟน)
*thoh-rá-sàp áep-pêrrn
(ai-fohn)*
Apple phones (iPhones)

9 โทรศัพท์มือถือ
*thoh-rá-sàp
mueh-thǔeh*
mobile phone

10 โทรออก
thoh-àwk
**to make a
phone call**

11 รับสาย
ráp-sǎay
**to receive a
phone call**

Additional Vocabulary

24 เบอร์โทรศัพท์
berr thoh-rá-sàp
telephone number

25 เครือข่าย;
อินเทอร์เน็ต
*khruea-khàay;
in-terr-nèt*
network; Internet

26 ภาษาอินเทอร์เน็ต
phaa-sǎa in-terr-nèt
Internet language

27 ส่งข้อความ
sòng khâw-khwaam
texting

28 ภาษาสแลงใน
อินเทอร์เน็ต
*phaa-sǎa sà-laehng
nai in-terr-nèt*
Internet slang

29 บัตรเติมเงิน
bàt term-ngerrn
top-up cards

30 สายชาร์จโทรศัพท์
*sǎay cháat thoh-
rá-sàp*
phone charger

31 โทรศัพท์ทางไกล
*thoh-rá-sàp thaang-
glai*
long distance call

32 รหัสประเทศ
rá-hàt prà-thêht
country code

33 รหัสพื้นที่
rá-hàt phúehn-thîi
area code

34 ซิมการ์ด
sim gáat
SIM card

12 สัญญาณแรง
săn-yaan raehng
strong signal

13 สัญญาณอ่อน
săn-yaan àwn
weak signal

14 เซลฟี่
sehl-fĭi
selfie

15 วีฟี่
wii-fĭi
wefie

16 ยูทูป
yuu-thúup
YouTube

17 อินสตาแกรม
in-sà-taa-graem
Instagram

18 เฟซบุ๊ก
fét-búk
Facebook

19 กูเกิล
guu-gêrrn
Google

20 ไลน์
laai
Line

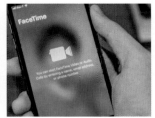

21 เฟซไทม์
fét-thaam
FaceTime

22 แอปเปิล
áep-pêrrn
Apple

23 ไมโครซอฟท์
mai-khroh-sáwp
Microsoft

Some common telephone phrases:

35 สวัสดีค่ะ/ครับ (name) พูดค่ะ/ครับ
Sà-wàt-dii khá/khráp? (name) phûut khá/khráp.
Hello? This is (name).

36 ขอพูดกับ (name)
Khăw phûut gàp (name) ?
May I speak to (name)?

37 ช่วยบอกเขาให้โทรกลับ ฉัน/ผม ด้วย
Chûay bàwk khăo hâi thoh-glàp chăn/phŏm dâuy.
Please ask him/her to return my call.

38 สะดวกคุยไหม
Sà-dûak khui maí?
Is it convenient to talk now?

39 ช่วยพูดดังขึ้นอีกหน่อยได้ไหม
Chûay phûut dang khûen ìik-nòy dâi-mái?
Could you speak up?

40 ขอโทษ คุณโทรผิดเบอร์
Khăw-thôht, khun thoh-phìt berr.
Sorry, you dialed the wrong number.

41 รอสักครู่นะคะ/ครับ
Raw sàk-khrûu ná-khá/khráp.
Please wait a moment.

42 ฝากข้อความไว้นะคะ/ครับ
Fàak khâw-khwaam wái ná-khá/khráp.
Please leave a message.

43 ไม่ทราบว่าใครโทรมาคะ/ครับ
Mâi-sâap wâa khrai thoh maa khá/khráp?
Who's calling, please?

44 ช่วยพูดช้าๆ หน่อยได้ไหม
Chûay phûut cháa cháa nòy dâi-mái?
Could you speak a little slower?

25

ที่ทำงาน
Thîi tham-ngaan
At work

1 ทนายความ
thá-naay-khwaam
lawyer

2 ผู้พิพากษา
phûu-phí-phâak-săa
judge

9 สถาปนิก
sà-thăa-pà-ník
architect

10 พนักงานรับโทรศัพท์
phá-nák-ngaan ráp thoh-rá-sàp
telephone operator

3 นักการเงิน
nák-gaan-ngerrn
financier

4 วิศวกร
wít-sà-wá-gawn
engineer

15 สำนักงาน
săm-nák-ngaan
office

16 เพื่อนร่วมงาน
phûean rûam-ngaan
colleague

5 นักบัญชี
nák-ban-chii
accountant

6 เภสัชกร
pheh-sàt-chá-gawn
pharmacist

7 ศิลปิน
sĭn-lá-pin
artist

8 นักดนตรี
nák-don-trii
musician

17 ผู้จัดการ
phûu-jàt-gaan
manager

18 เลขานุการ
leh-khăa-nú-gaan
secretary

11 เชฟ
chép
chef

12 ช่างภาพ
châang-phâap
photographer

13 นักบิน
nák-bin
pilot

14 ทันตแพทย์; หมอฟัน
than-tà-phâeht (formal);
măw-fan (informal)
dentist

19 พนักงานดับเพลิง
phá-nák-ngaan
dàp-phlerrng
firefighter

20 เกษตรกร; ชาวนา
gà-sèht-tà-gawn
(formal); chaaw-naa
(informal)
farmer

Additional Vocabulary

21 บริษัท
baw-rí-sàt
company

22 ผู้ประกอบการ
phûu-prà-gàwp-gaan
entrepreneur

23 ตรวจสอบ
trùat-sàwp
to inspect

24 ไปทำงาน
pai tham-ngaan
going to work

25 ทำงาน
tham-ngaan
work

26 พนักงาน
phá-nák-ngaan
employee

27 ฝึกงาน
fùek-ngaan
**apprentice;
to intern**

28 ทำงานเป็นกะ
*tham-ngaan
pen gà*
shift work

29 ทำงานล่วงเวลา
*tham-ngaan
lûang weh-laa*
**to work
overtime**

30 ผู้ให้บริการ
phûu hâi baw-rí-gaan
**service
provider**

31 วิธี
wí-thii
method

32 โอกาส
oh-gàat
opportunity

33 ตำแหน่ง
tam-nàehng
position

34 เสมอ
sà-mĕrr
always

35 คุณทำงานด้านไหน ฉัน/ผมทำงานที่โรงพยาบาล
*Khun tham-ngaan dâan năi? Chăn/Phŏm tham-
ngaan thîi rohng-phá-yaa-baan.*
What sort of work do you do? I work in a hospital.

36 ฉัน/ผม เป็นหมอฝึกหัด
Chăn/Phŏm pen măw fùek-hàt.
I'm training to be a doctor.

37 ฉันไปทำงาน 8.45 น. ทุกเช้า
Chăn pai tham-ngaan pàeht mohng sìi-sìp-hâa naa-thii thúk cháo.
I go to work at 8:45 a.m. every morning.

59

ดนตรีและการเต้นรำ

Don-trii láe gaan tên-ram

26 | Music and dance

1 กีตาร์
gii-tâa
guitar

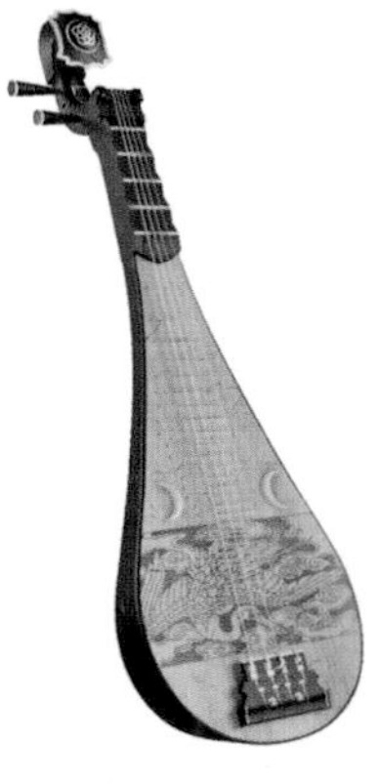

2 พิณ
phin
three-stringed lute

3 ไวโอลิน
wai-oh-lin
violin

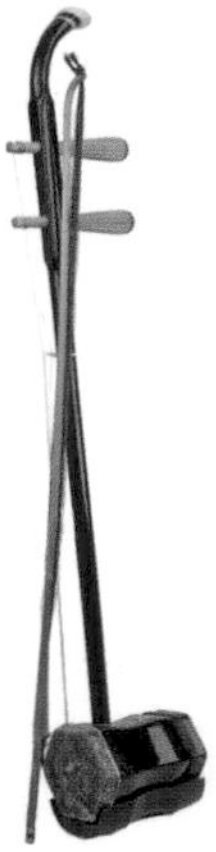

4 ซอด้วง
saw-dûang
higher two-string fiddle

5 เต้น
tên
to dance

6 กลอง
glawng
drums

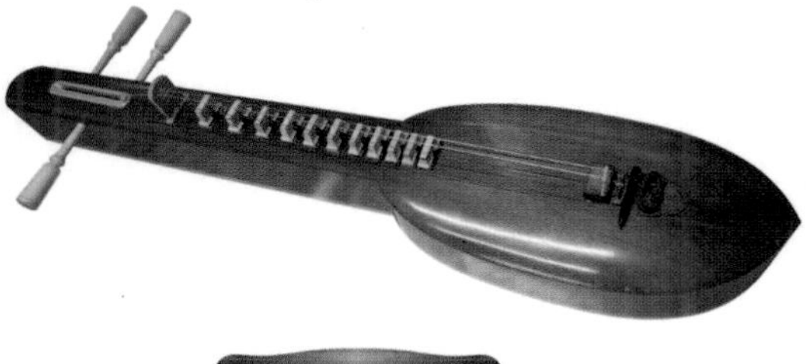

7 จะเข้
jà-khêh
crocodile-shaped fretted floor zither

8 เปียโน
pia-noh
piano

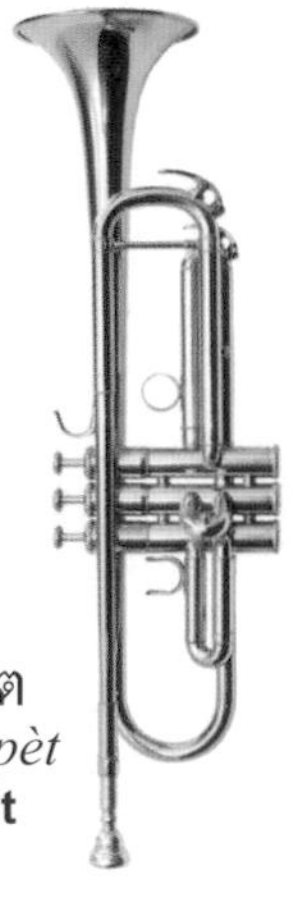

9 ทรัมเป็ต
thram-pèt
trumpet

10 ขลุ่ย
khlùy
flute

11 คาราโอเกะ
khaa-raa-oh-gè
karaoke

12 ร้องเพลง
ráwng-phlehng
to sing

13 นักร้อง
nák-ráwng
singer

20 เพลิดเพลิน; สนุก
phlêrrt-phlerrn;
sà-nùk
to appreciate;
to enjoy

21 ดนตรี
don-trii
music

22 เต้นรำ
tên-ram
dance (performance
art)

23 แสดง
sà-daehng
to perform

24 รายการ
raay-gaan
program

25 เพลงป๊อบ
phleng páwp
pop music

26 เล่นดนตรีเครื่องสาย
lêhn don-trii
krûeang-sǎay
to play a string
instrument

27 หูฟัง
hǔu-fang
earphones

28 เล่น (ดนตรี)
lêhn (don-trii)
to perform (on a
musical instrument)

29 วงดนตรี
wong don-trii
band

30 วงออเคสตรา
wong aw-khes-tráa
orchestra

31 งานอดิเรก
ngaan à-dì-rèhk
hobby

32 มีชื่อเสียง
mii chûeh sǐang
famous

33 แสดงออก
sà-daehng àwk
to express

14 คอนเสิร์ต
khawn-sèrrt
concert

15 คนดู
khon-duu
audience

16 โขน
khǒhn
Thai masked
dance drama

17 ตัวพระ; ตัวนาง
tua-phrá;
tua-naang
actor; actress

18 เชลโล
chehl-lôh
cello

34 คุณเล่นกีตาร์ได้ไหม
Khun lêhn gii-tâa dâi-mái?
Can you play the guitar?

19 นักร้องเพลงป๊อป
nák-ráwng phleng páwp
pop group

35 คุณชอบเพลงแบบไหน
Khun châwp phlehng bàehp nǎi?
What kind of music do you like?

27

ไปหาหมอ

Pai hăa măw

Seeing a doctor

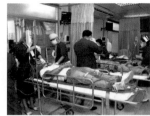

4 หมอ; แพทย์
măw (informal);
phâeht (formal)
doctor

3 พยาบาล
phá-yaa-baan
nurse

5 คนไข้
khon khâi
patient

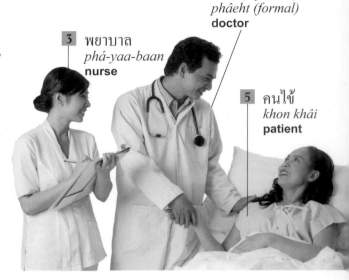

1 โรงพยาบาล
rohng phá-yaa-baan
hospital

2 ห้องฉุกเฉิน
hâwng chùk-chěrrn
emergency room

6 เจาะเลือด
jàw lûeat
to draw blood

7 ตรวจเลือด
trùat lûeat
blood test

8 การตรวจแล็บ
gaan trùat làep
laboratory test

9 ความดันเลือด
khwaam-dan lûeat
blood pressure

10 เป็นหวัด
pen wàt
to catch a cold

11 ไอ
ai
to cough

12 ไข้
khâi
fever

13 ไม่สบาย
mâi sà-baay
to fall sick

14 กินยา
gin yaa
to take medicine

15 ยา
yaa
medicine

16 ยาเม็ด
yaa-mét
pills

17 ฉีดยา
chìit-yaa
injection

18 ห้องตรวจ
hâwng trùat
doctor's
consultation room

19 ห้องรอพบแพทย์
hâwng raw phóp phâeht
waiting room

20 การนัดหมาย
gaan nát-măay
appointment

21 รถพยาบาล
rót phá-yaa-baan
ambulance

22 ทันตกรรม
than-tà-gam
dentistry

23 อายุรกรรมทั่วไป
aa-yú-rá-gam thûa-pai
general medicine

24 ศัลยกรรมทั่วไป
săn-yá-gam thûa-pai
general surgery

25 หู จมูก และคอ
hŭu, jà-mùuk, láe khaw
ear, nose, and throat

26 กุมารเวชศาสตร์
gù-maan wêht-chá-sàat
pediatrics

27 นรีเวชวิทยา
ná-rii-wêht wít-thá-yaa
gynecology

28 จักษุวิทยา
jàk-sù wít-thá-yaa
ophthalmology

29 ผิวหนังวิทยา
phĭw-năng wít-thá-yaa
dermatology

30 มะเร็งวิทยา
má-reng wít-thá-yaa
oncology

31 กายภาพบำบัด
gaay-yá-phâap bam-bàt
physiotherapy

32 ประสาทวิทยา
prà-sàat wít-thá-yaa
neurology

33 รังสีวิทยา
rang-sĭi wít-thá-yaa
radiology

34 อุบัติเหตุ
ù-bàt-tì-hèht
accident

35 ใบสั่งยา
bai-sàng-yaa
prescription

36 ยาฆ่าเชื้อ
yaa-khâ-chûea
antiseptic

37 ยาทา
yaa-thaa
ointment

38 แผล
phlăeh
wound; cut

39 ฉุกเฉิน
chùk-chĕrrn
emergency

40 บาดเจ็บ
bàat-jèp
hurts

41 เหนื่อย
nùeay
tired; worn out

42 รู้สึก
rúu-sùek
to feel

43 จาก
jàak
from

44 หลายครั้ง
lăay khráng
several times

45 กังวล; เป็นห่วง
gang-won; pen-hùang
anxious; worried

46 พบ
phóp
to discover

47 รู้สึกมั่นใจ
rúu-sùek mân-jai
to feel reassured

48 กังวลเรื่อง
gang-won rûeang
to be concerned about

49 เกี่ยวข้องกับ
gìaw-khâwng gàp
pertaining to

50 หวัง
wăng
hope

51 สำคัญ
săm-khan
important

52 หลัก
làk
main

53 ชุดปฐมพยาบาล
chút pà-thŏm-phá-yaa-baan
first aid kit

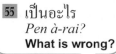

55 เป็นอะไร
Pen à-rai?
What is wrong?

54 ผ้าพันแผล
phâa phan phlăeh
bandage

57 ฉัน/ผมรู้สึกไม่สบาย
Chăn/Phŏm rúu-sùek mâi sà-baay.
I am not feeling well.

58 ฉัน/ผมอยากไปหาหมอ
Chăn/Phŏm yàak pai hăa măw.
I would like to see a doctor.

59 คุณนัดหมายไว้หรือเปล่า
Khun nát-măay wái rúe-plào?
Do you have an appointment?

56 ผมมีไข้และเจ็บคอ
Phŏm pen-khâi gàp jèp-khaw.
I have a fever and a sore throat.

ปกป้องสิ่งแวดล้อม
28
Pòk-pâwng sìng-wâeht-láwm
Protecting our environment

1 สวน
sŭan
garden

2 ดอกไม้
dàwk-mái
flower

6 รถยนต์ไฟฟ้า
rót-yon fai-fáa
electric car

3 สวนสาธารณะ
sŭan săa-thaa-rá-ná
park

4 มลพิษ
mon-lá-phít
pollution

5 หญ้า
yâa
grass

7 มหาสมุทร
má-hăa sà-mùt
ocean

8 แม่น้ำ
mâeh-náam
river

9 พลังงานแสงอาทิตย์
*phá-lang-ngaan
săehng-aa-thít*
solar energy

10 เงียบ
ngîap
quiet

44 อากาศที่นี่สดชื่นจริงๆ
Aa-gàat thîi-nîi sòt-chûehn jing-jing!
The air here is really fresh!

12 พลังงานลม
phá-lang-ngaan lom
wind power

11 อากาศ
aa-kàat
air

13 แผงกั้นทราย
phǎehng gân saay
sand break

14 ป่า
pàa
forest

16 ก๊าซธรรมชาติ
gáat tham-má-châat
natural gas

17 พลังงานนิวเคลียร์
phá-lang-ngaan niw-khlia
nuclear energy

15 ต้นไม้
tón-mái
tree

45 คุณรีไซเคิลไหม
Khun rii-sai-khêrrn mái?
Do you recycle?

46 ฉันรีไซเคิลแก้ว กระดาษกับพลาสติก
Chǎn rii-sai-khêrrn gâehw grà-dàat gàp phláat-sà-tìk.
I recycle glass, paper and plastic.

Additional Vocabulary

18 สะอาด
sà-àat
clean

19 พืช
phûeht
plant

20 การรีไซเคิล
gaan rii-sai-khêrrn
recycling

21 พลังงานสะอาด
phá-lang-ngaan sà-àat
clean energy

22 น้ำมัน
náam-man
oil

23 ถ่านหิน
thàan-hǐn
coal

24 คุณภาพอากาศ
khun-ná-phâap aa-kàat
air quality

25 ดัชนี
dàt-chá-nii
index

26 น้ำ
náam
water

27 ทำความสะอาด
tham khwaam-sà-àat
clean

28 สิ่งแวดล้อม
sìng-wâeht-láwm
environment

29 หน้ากาก
nâa-gàak
mask

30 การเปลี่ยนแปลง
gaan plìan-plaehng
changes

31 พื้นดิน
phûehn din
earth; ground

32 โดย
dohy
by

33 เพราะว่า
phràw wâa
because of

34 จุดประสงค์เพื่อ
jùt-prà-sǒng phûea
for the purpose of

35 เสร็จเรียบร้อย
sèt rîap-róy
complete

36 ทำสำเร็จ
tham sǎm-rèt
to accomplish

37 ส่งผลกระทบ
sòng phǒn-grà-thóp
to affect

38 แต่
tàeh
but

39 อย่างไรก็ตาม
yàang-rai gâw-taam
however

40 แน่นอน
nâeh-nawn
of course

41 ถ้า
thâa
if

42 แม้ว่า
máeh-wâa
although

43 เป็นผลมาจาก
pen phǒn maa-jàak
as a result of

29 อาณาจักรสัตว์

Aa-naa-jàk sàt

The animal kingdom

1 สวนสัตว์
sŭan-sàt
zoo

2 ม้าลาย
máa-laay
zebra

3 ยีราฟ
yii-ráap
giraffe

---

39 สัตว์ตัวนี้เล็กกว่าตัวนั้น
Sàt tua-níi lék-gwàa tua-nán.
This animal is smaller than that one.

40 คุณชอบไปสวนสัตว์ไหม
Khun châwp pai sŭan-sàt mái?
Do you like going to the zoo?

41 มีสัตว์หลายตัวในสวนสัตว์
Mii sàt lăay tua nai sŭan-sàt.
There are many animals in the zoo.

4 เสือ
sŭea
tiger

5 สิงโต
sing-toh
lion

6 หมี
mĭi
bear

10 ไดโนเสาร์
dai-noh-săo
dinosaur

7 ลิง
ling
monkey

8 กอริลลา
gaw-rin-lâa
gorilla

9 หมีแพนด้า
mĭi phaehn-dâa
panda

11 แพะ
pháe
goat

12 แกะ
gàe
sheep

13 วัว
wua
cow

Additional Vocabulary

29 เหลือเกิน
lŭea-gerrn
how (wonderful, etc.)

30 กลัว
glua
to be afraid

31 น่ารัก
nâa-rák
cute; adorable

32 มัน
man
it

33 มากที่สุด
mâak thîi-sùt
extremely

34 เหมือนกัน
mŭean-gan
same; identical

35 คล้าย
khláay
to resemble

36 ปรากฏ
praa-gòt
to appear

37 กล้า
glâa
to dare

38 แปลก
plàehk
strange

14 ช้าง
cháang
elephant

15 ม้า
máa
horse

‑6 หมาป่า
măa-pàa
wolf

17 งู
nguu
snake

13 นกยูง
nók-yuung
peacock

19 ไก่
gài
chicken

20 นก
nók
bird

21 หมา
măa
dog

22 แมว
maehw
cat

23 มังกร
mang-gawn
dragon

24 ยุง
yung
mosquito

25 แมลงวัน
má-laehng wan
housefly

26 ผึ้ง
phûeng
bee

27 ผีเสื้อ
phĭi-sûea
butterfly

28 ปลา
plaa
fish

มาออกกำลังกายกัน
Maa àwk-gam-lang-gaay gan!
Let's keep fit!

30

1 ปิงปอง
ping-pawng
table tennis

2 เล่นฟุตบอล
lêhn fút-bawn
to play soccer

3 รักบี้
rák-bîi
rugby

4 ปีนเขา
piin kăo
mountain climbing

5 แบดมินตัน
bàeht-min-tân
badminton

6 ออกกำลังกาย
àwk-gam-lang-gaay
to exercise

7 เบสบอล
bêhs-bawn
baseball

8 กีฬา
gii-laa
sports

9 รองเท้ากีฬา
rawng-tháo gii-laa
sports shoes

11 วิ่ง
wîng
running

12 วิ่งระยะไกล
wîng rá-yá-glai
long-distance running

13 จักรยาน
jàk-grà-yaan
bicycle

10 วิ่งเร็วระยะสั้น
wîng rew rá-yá-sân
sprint

14 ปั่น
pàn
to cycle

17 กอล์ฟ
gàwp
golf

18 สเก็ตน้ำแข็ง
sà-gét náam-khăeng
ice-skating

19 เล่นสกี
lêhn sà-gii
skiing

15 การแข่งขัน
gaan khàehng-khăn
competition

15 เส้นชัย
sêhn-chai
finish line

20 พายเรือ
phaay-ruea
rowing

21 ว่ายน้ำ
wâay-náam
swimming

Additional Vocabulary

27 เสื้อกีฬา
sûea gii-laa
sports shirt; sweatshirt

28 รองเท้าผ้าใบ
rawng-tháo phâa-bai
sneakers

29 ลูกบอล
lúuk-bawn
ball

30 แข็งแรง
khăeng-raehng
healthy

22 วอลเลย์บอล
wawn-lêh-bawn
volleyball

23 เดิน
derrn
walking

24 เทนนิส
thehn-nít
tennis

25 ไม้
mái
racket

31 คุณชอบออกกำลังกายไหม
Khun châwp àwk-gam-lang-gaay mái?
Do you like to exercise?

32 คุณเล่นกีฬาอะไร
Khun lêhn gii-laa à-rai?
What sports do you play?

33 ฉัน/ผมชอบวิ่งช้าๆ กับเล่นบาสเก็ตบอล
Chăn/Phŏm châwp wing cháa cháa gàp lêhn báas-gét-bawn.
I like to jog and play basketball.

26 เล่นบาสเก็ตบอล
lêhn báas-gét-bawn
play basketball

31 คุณชอบเดินทางไหม
Khun châwp derrn-thaang mái?
Do you like to travel?

3 นักเดินทาง
nák derrn-thaang
traveler

4 กระเป๋าเดินทาง
grà-pǎo derrn-thaang
luggage; suitcase

1 โรงแรม
rohng-raehm
hotel

2 แผนที่
phǎehn-thîi
map

5 ไกด์นำเที่ยว
gái nam thîaw
tour guide

6 สถานที่ท่องเที่ยว
sà-thǎan-thîi thâwng-thîaw
tourist attraction

7 หนังสือเดินทาง
nǎng-sǔeh derrn-thaang
passport

8 บัตรที่นั่ง
bàt thîi-nâng
boarding pass

9 เดินทางโดยเครื่องบิน
derrn-thaang dohy khrûeang-bin
travel by airplane

10 เดินทางโดยรถไฟ
derrn-thaang dohy rót-fai
travel by rail

11 บนเรือสำราญ
bon ruea sǎm-raan
on a cruise

12 บนรถทัวร์
bon rót-thua
on a coach

13 ร้านขายของที่ระลึก
ráan khǎay khǎwng-thîi-rá-lúek
souvenir shop

14 กล้อง
glâwng
camera

15 รูปถ่าย
rûup-thàay
photograph

16 การเดินทาง
gaan derrn-thaang
a trip

17 เดินทาง
derrn-thaang
to travel

18 วันหยุด
wan yùt
vacation

19 ตั๋วเครื่องบิน
tŭa khrûeang-bin
plane ticket

20 เงินตรา
ngerrn-traa
currency

21 วีซ่า
wii-sâa
visa

22 การฉีดวัคซีน
gaan chìit wák-siin
vaccination

23 ศุลกากร
sŭn-lá-gaa-gawn
customs

24 การจองโรงแรม
gaan-jawng rohng-raehm
hotel reservation

25 เกสท์เฮ้าส์
gêhs-háo
guesthouse

26 โรงแรม
rohng-raehm
lodge

27 ที่พักเยาวชน
thîi-phák yao-wá-chon
youth hostel

28 ไวไฟฟรี
waai-faai frii
free wifi

29 คู่มือท่องเที่ยว
khûu-mueh thâwng-thîaw
travel guidebook

30 ชมวิว
chom-wiw
sightseeing

31 โปสการ์ด;
ไปรษณียบัตร
*póht-sà-gáat
(informal);
prai-sà-nii-yá-bàt*
postcard

32 พิพิธภัณฑ์
phí-phít-thá-phan
museum

33 ชายหาด
chaay-hàat
beach

34 อนุสาวรีย์
à-nú-săa-wá-rii
monument

35 สถานีรถไฟ
sà-thăa-nii rót-fai
train station

36 สนามบิน
sà-năam bin
airport

37 ศูนย์เรือนำเที่ยว
sŭun ruea nam-thîaw
cruise center

38 ร้านอาหาร
ráan aa-hăan
restaurant

39 พบ
phóp
to find

40 ขึ้น
khûen
to take

41 พบกับ
phóp-gàp
to come across

42 ให้ความสนใจกับ
hâi khwaam-sŏn-jai gàp
to pay attention to

43 รับรู้
ráp-rúu
to become aware of

44 ตัวแทนการท่องเที่ยว
tua-thaehn gaan-thâwng-thîaw
travel agency

45 ศูนย์ข้อมูลการท่องเที่ยว
sŭun khâw-muun gaan-thâwng-thîaw
tourist information center

46 วันหยุดคุณชอบไปเที่ยวที่ไหน
Wan-yùt khun châwp pai thîaw thîi-năi?
Where do you like to go on vacation?

47 ฉันชอบไปภูเก็ต
Chăn châwp pai Phuket.
I like to go to Phuket.

48 ซื้อตั๋วรถไฟชั้นสองไปกลับเชียงใหม่
Súeh tŭa rót-fai chán săwng pai-glàp Chiang Mai.
I'd like a second class return train ticket to Chiang Mai.

49 เขาเดินทางรอบโลก
Khăo derrn-thaang râwp lôhk.
He made a round-the-world trip.

50 ฉัน/ผมชอบบินกับสายการบินเดิมเพื่อสะสมไมล์
Chăn/Phŏm châwp bin gàp săay-gaan-bin derrm phûea sà-sŏm mai.
I like to fly on the same airline to get mileage points.

ประเทศทั่วโลก

32
Prà-thêht thûa lôhk
Countries of the world

1 ประเทศในเอเชียตะวันออกเฉียงใต้
prà-thêht nai eh-chia tà-wan-àwk chǐang tâi
Countries in Southeast Asia

2 ประเทศไทย
prà-thêht Thai
Thailand

3 เมียนมาร์
mian-mâa
Myanmar

4 เวียดนาม
wîat-naam
Vietnam

5 ฟิลิปปินส์
fí-líp-pin
Philippines

6 ลาว
laaw
Laos

7 กัมพูชา
gam-phuu-chaa
Cambodia

8 มาเลเซีย
maa-leh-sia
Malaysia

9 บรูไน
briu-nai
Brunei

10 สิงคโปร์
sǐng-khá-poh
Singapore

11 อินโดนีเซีย
in-doh-nii-sia
Indonesia

12 ติมอร์ตะวันออก
tì-maw tà-wan-àwk
East Timor

30 เราตั้งใจจะจัดพิธีแต่งงานที่ประเทศไทย
Rao tâng-jai jà jàt phí-thii tàehng-ngaan thîi prà-thêht Thai.
We intend to hold our wedding ceremony in Thailand.

31 คุณมาจากประเทศอะไร ฉัน/ผมเป็นคนอเมริกัน
Khun maa jàak prà-thêht à-rai? Chǎn/Phǒm pen khon À-meh-rí-gan.
What country are you from? I am American.

15 เจ็ดทวีปในโลก
jèt thá-wîip nai lôhk
Seven continents of the world

14 ทวีปอเมริกาเหนือ
thá-wîip à-meh-ri-gaa nŭea
North America

15 ทวีปอเมริกาใต้
thá-wîip à-meh-ri-gaa tâi
South America

16 ทวีปยุโรป
thá-wîip yú-ròhp
Europe

17 ทวีปแอฟริกา
thá-wîip àehp-frí-gaa
Africa

18 ทวีปเอเชีย
thá-wîip eh-chia
Asia

19 ทวีปออสเตรเลีย
thá-wîip àws-treh-lia
Australia

20 ทวีปแอนตาร์กติกา
thá-wîip aehn-tàak-tì-gâa
Antarctica

21 ญี่ปุ่น
yîi-pùn
Japan

22 เกาหลี
gao-lĭi
Korea

23 จีน
jiin
China

24 สหรัฐอเมริกา
sà-hà-rát à-meh-rí-gaa
USA

25 อินเดีย
in-dia
India

26 ออสเตรเลีย
áws-treh-lia
Australia

แคนาดา *khaeh-naa-daa* Canada
เดนมาร์ก *den-màak* Denmark
ฟินแลนด์ *fin-laehn* Finland
เยอรมัน *yerr-rá-man* Germany
เกาะบริเตนใหญ่ *gàw-brí-ten-yài* Great Britain
ไอร์แลนด์ *ai-laehn* Ireland
ลักเซมเบิร์ก *lák-sehm-bèrrk* Luxembourg
เนเธอร์แลนด์ *neh-thêrr-laehn* Netherlands

27 อิตาลี
i-taa-lîi
Italy

นิวซีแลนด์ *niw-sii-laehn* New Zealand
นอร์เวย์ *naw-weh* Norway
โปแลนด์ *poh-laehn* Poland
รัสเซีย *rát-sia* Russia
สวีเดน *sà-wii-den* Sweden
สวิตเซอร์แลนด์ *sà-wít-ser-laehn* Switzerland
นครรัฐวาติกัน *ná-khawn waa-tì-gan* Vatican

28 แผนที่โลก
phăehn-thîi lôhk
globe

29 โลก
lôhk
world

33

ภาษาต่างประเทศ
Phaa-săa tàang-prà-thêht
Foreign languages

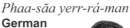

> Guten Tag!

> Hello!

> Bonjour!

> привет

4 ภาษาเยอรมัน
Phaa-săa yerr-rá-man
German

1 ภาษาอังกฤษ
Phaa-săa Àng-grìt
English

2 ภาษาฝรั่งเศส
Phaa-săa Fà-ràng-sèht
French

3 ภาษารัสเซีย
Phaa-săa Rát-sia
Russian

> Ciao!

> ¡Hola!

5 ภาษาอิตาลี
Phaa-săa Ì-taa-lîi
Italian

6 ภาษาสเปน
Phaa-săa Sà-pehn
Spanish

> Merhaba!

> こんにちは

> مرحبا

7 ภาษาตุรกี
Phaa-săa Tù-rá-gii
Turkish

8 ภาษาญี่ปุ่น
Phaa-săa Yîi-pùn
Japanese

9 ภาษาอาหรับ
Phaa-săa Aa-ràp
Arabic

Χαίρετε

10 ภาษากรีก
Phaa-săa Grìik
Greek

שלום

11 ภาษาฮิบรู
Phaa-săa Hí-bruu
Hebrew

Xin chào!

12 ภาษาเวียดนาม
Phaa-săa Wîat-naam
Vietnamese

สวัสดี

นมสเต

13 ภาษาฮินดี
Phaa-săa Hin-dii
Hindi

Apa kabar

14 ภาษาอินโดนีเซีย
Phaa-săa In-doh-nii-sia
Indonesian

15 ภาษาไทย
Phaa-săa Thai
Thai

안녕하세요

16 ภาษาเกาหลี
Phaa-săa Gao-lĭi
Korean

Kamusta

17 ภาษาตากาล็อก
Phaa-săa Taa-gaa-láwk
Tagalog

Olá!

18 ภาษาโปรตุเกส
Phaa-săa Proh-tù-gèht
Portuguese

你好！

19 ภาษาจีนกลาง
Phaa-săa Jiin-glaang
Mandarin Chinese

20 คุณพูดภาษาอะไร
Khun phûut phaa-săa à-rai?
What is your mother tongue?

21 คุณพูดกี่ภาษา
Khun phûut gìi phaa-săa?
How many languages do you speak?

คุณชอบอาหารไทยไหม

34

Khun châwp aa-hǎan thai mái

Do you like Thai food?

1 ร้านอาหารไทย
ráan aa-hǎan Thai
Thai restaurant

2 พนักงานเสิร์ฟ; เด็กเสิร์ฟ
phá-nák-ngaan-sèrrp (formal);
dèk-sèrrp (informal)
waiter; waitress

3 พ่อครัว; แม่ครัว; เชฟ
phâw-khrua (male);
mâeh-khrua (female);
chéhp
cook; chef

4 เมนู
meh-nuu
menu

5 ผัดไทย
phàt-thai
fried noodle (pad Thai)

6 ข้าวผัด
khâaw phàt
fried rice

7 ขนมปัง
khà-nǒm-pang
bread

8 ตะเกียบ
tà-gìap
chopsticks

13 ส้อม
sâwm
fork

14 มีด
mîit
knife

9 ถ้วย
thûay
bowl

10 ข้าว
khâaw
cooked rice

11 ข้าวสีขาว
khâaw sǐi-khǎaw
white rice

12 จาน
jaan
plate

15 ช้อน
cháwn
spoon

16 แกงเขียวหวาน
gaeng khǐaw wǎan
green curry (usually sweet and mildly spicy)

17 ต้มยำกุ้ง
tôm-yam gûng
spicy shrimp soup

18 พะแนงไก่
phá-naeng gài
red curry paste with chicken

19 ไก่ผัดเม็ดมะม่วง
gài phàt mét-má-mûang
chicken with cashews

Additional Vocabulary

26 น้ำซุป; แกง
náam súp (no meat); gaehng (with meat)
soup

20 ส้มตำ
sôm-tam
green papaya spicy salad

21 ไก่ย่าง
gài-yâang
grilled chicken

22 ข้าวเหนียว
khâaw-nǐaw
sticky rice

27 มังสวิรัติ
mang-sà-wí-rát
vegetarian

28 สั่ง
sàng
to order

23 ไข่เจียวหมูสับ
khài-jiaw mǔu-sàp
omelet with minced pork

24 ผัดกะเพราหมู
phàt gà-phrao mǔu
minced pork with sweet basil

25 ก๋วยเตี๋ยวเนื้อ
gǔay-tǐaw núea
beef noodle soup

29 ตัวเลือก
tua-lûeak
choice

30 พิเศษ
phí-sèht
special

31 ด้วย
dûay
also; too

34 ทุกคนชอบกินอาหารไทย
Túk-khon châwp gin aa-hǎan thai.
Everyone likes to eat Thai food.

35 ฉันอยากชวนคุณมากินอาหารเย็นคืนนี้
Chǎn yàak chuan khun maa gin aa-hǎan yen khuehn-níi.
I'm inviting you for dinner tonight.

36 ดีมากเลย ผมอยากกินอาหารไทย
Dii-mâak loei! Phǒm yàak gin aa-hǎan Thai.
That's great! I want to eat Thai food.

32 บางที
bang-thii
perhaps

33 เกือบ
gùeap
almost

37 น้อง.....คะ
Náwng.....khá
Miss...(waitress)

77

อาหารตะวันตกยอดนิยม
Aa-hăan tà-wan-tòk yâwt-ní-yom
Popular Western foods

1 ฮอทดอก
háwt-dàwk
hot dog

2 แซนด์วิช
saehn-wít
sandwich

3 พิซซ่า
phít-sâa
pizza

4 พาสต้า; สปาเก็ตตี้
pháas-tâa; sà-paa-gét-tîi
pasta; spaghetti

5 โดนัท
doh-nát
donuts

6 ขนมปังฝรั่งเศส
*khà-nŏm-pang
fà-ràng-sèht*
baguette

7 ไอศกรีม; ไอติม
*ai-sà-khriim (formal);
ai-tim (informal)*
ice cream

8 พุดดิ้ง
phút-dîng
pudding

9 ลาซานญ่า
laa-saan-yâa
lasagne

10 ไก่งวง
gài-nguang
turkey

11 พายแอปเปิล
phaay áep-pêrrn
apple pie

12 แฮม
haehm
ham

15 สเต็ก
sà-ték
steak

13 สลัด
sà-làt
salad

16 ไส้กรอก
sâi-gràwk
sausage

14 มันฝรั่งบด
man-fà-ràng bòt
mashed potatoes

17 อาหารเช้าแบบตะวันตก
aa-hăn cháo bàehp tà-wan-tòk
Western breakfast

18 น้ำผลไม้
náam phŏn-lá-mái
fruit juice

19 กาแฟ
gaa-faeh
coffee

20 เบคอน; แฮมรมควัน
beh-khâwn; haehm rom-khwan
bacon; smoked ham

21 ไข่ดาวไม่สุก
khài-daaw mâi sùk
sunny side up eggs

22 ขนมปังปิ้ง
khà-nŏm-pang pîng
toast

ร้านอาหารฟาสต์ฟู้ดยอดนิยมในประเทศไทย
Ráan-aa-hăn fáat-fúut yâwt-ní-yom nai prà-thêt thai
Some popular fast food chains in Thailand

สตาร์บัคส์
Sa-taa-bák
Starbucks

แมคโดนัลด์
Máek-doh-nâel
McDonald's

สเวนเซ่นส์
Sà-wen-sên
Swensen's

เดอะ พิซซ่า คอมปะนี
Dèr Phít-sâa Kham-pà-nii
The Pizza Company

เคเอฟซี
Kheh-éhp-sii
Kentucky Fried Chicken

ซิซซ์เล่อร์
Sís-lêrr
Sizzler

23 เค้ก
khéhk
cake

24 ชีส
chíis
cheese

25 ธัญพืช
than-yá-phûeht
cereal

26 ข้าวโอ๊ต; ข้าวโอ๊ตแผ่น
khâaw óht; khâaw óht phàehn
oatmeal; rolled oats

Additional Vocabulary

29 อาหารแบบตะวันตก
aa-hăn bàehp tà-wan-tòk
Western-style food

30 อร่อย
à-ròy
tasty; delicious

31 บาร์บีคิว
baa-bii-khiw
barbecue

32 ย่าง; อบ
yâang; òp
to roast; to bake

33 แพนเค้ก
phaehn-khéhk
pancakes

34 เนย; ครีม
noei; khriim
butter; cream

35 โยเกิร์ต
yoh-gèrrt
yogurt

36 ซอสมะเขือเทศ
sáwt má-khŭea-thêht
ketchup; tomato sauce

37 แมคโดนัลด์เป็นร้านอาหารฟาสต์ฟู้ดยอดนิยมในประเทศไทย
Máek-doh-nâel pen ráan-aa-hăn fáat-fúut yâwt-ní-yom nai prà-thêht Thai.
McDonalds is a popular fast food restaurant in Thailand.

38 เด็กทุกคนชอบแฮมเบอร์เกอร์กับมันฝรั่งทอด
Dèk thúk khon châwp haehm berr-gêrr gàp man fà-ràng thâwt.
All children like hamburgers and french fries.

39 คุณชอบอาหารไทยหรืออาหารตะวันตก
Khun châwp aa-hăn thai rŭeh aa-hăn tà-wan-tòk?
Do you prefer Thai food or Western food?

27 แฮมเบอร์เกอร์
haehm berr-gêrr
hamburger

28 มันฝรั่งทอด
man fà-ràng thâwt
french fries

เครื่องดื่ม

36

Khrûeang-dùehm

Drinks

1 เครื่องดื่ม
khrûeang-dùehm
beverage

2 น้ำแร่
náam râeh
mineral water

3 น้ำผลไม้
náam phŏn-lá-mái
fruit juice

4 น้ำส้ม
náam sôm
orange juice

5 นม
nom
milk

6 กาแฟ
gaa-faeh
coffee

7 ชา
chaa
tea

8 ชาเย็น
chaa-yen
iced tea

9 นมถั่วเหลือง
nom thùa-lŭeang
soy milk

10 โค้ก
khóhk
cola

11 น้ำประปา
náam prà-paa
tap water

15 เครื่องดื่มไม่มีน้ำตาล
khrûeang-dùehm mâi-mii náam-taan
diet drinks

12 น้ำ
náam
water

13 ดื่ม ; กินน้ำ
dùehm (formal);
gin náam (informal)
to drink

14 หิวน้ำ
dnáam
thirsty

16 เครื่องดื่มชูกำลัง
khrûeang-dùehm chuu gam-lang
energy drinks

17 เครื่องดื่มเกลือแร่
khrûeang-dùehm gluea-râeh
sports drinks

19 ไวน์แดง
waai-daehng
red wine

20 ไวน์ขาว
waai khǎaw
white wine

18 ค็อกเทล
kháwk-thehw
cocktails

21 เหล้า
lâo
whiskey

22 แชมเปญ
chaehm-pehn
Champagne

23 เหล้าขาว
lâo khǎaw
white spirit

24 เบียร์ไทย
bia thai
Thai beer

25 สาโท
sǎa-thoh
traditional rice wine (Sato)

26 เบียร์
bia
beer

Additional Vocabulary

27 โซดา
soh-daa
sodas

28 ตู้กดน้ำ
tûu gòt náam
office water dispenser

29 น้ำร้อน
náam ráwn
hot water

30 น้ำเย็น
náam yen
cold water; iced water

31 น้ำแข็งก้อน
náam khǎeng gâwn
ice cubes

32 แก้ว
gâehw
glass; cup

33 ขวด
khùat
bottle

34 ทุกวันเราควรดื่มน้ำกี่แก้ว
Thúk-wan rao khuan dùehm náam gìi gâehw?
How many glasses of water should people drink every day?

35 ถ้าคุณขับรถ อย่าดื่ม ถ้าคุณดื่ม อย่าขับรถ
Thâa khun khàp-rót yàa dùehm Thâa khun dùehm yàa khàp-rót.
If you drive, don't drink. If you drink, don't drive.

36 ฉัน/ผม อยากดื่มอะไรร้อนๆ
Chǎn/Phǒm yàak dùehm à-rai ráwn ráwn.
I want something hot to drink.

ผลไม้สด ถั่ว และธัญพืช

37

Phǒn-lá-mái sòt thùa láe than-yá-phûeht

Fresh fruits, nuts and grains

1 แอปเปิล
áep-pêrrn
apple

2 มะม่วง
má-mûang
mango

3 ส้ม
sôm
orange

4 ส้มจีน
sôm-jiin
mandarin orange

5 ลูกแพร์; สาลี่
lûuk phaeh; sǎa-lìi
pear

6 มะพร้าว
má-phráaw
coconut

7 กล้วย
glûay
banana

8 สับปะรด
sàp-pà-rót
pineapple

9 ลูกพีช
lûuk phíit
peach

10 มะละกอ
má-lá-gaw
papaya

11 เลมอน
leh-mâwn
lemon

12 มะนาว
má-naaw
lime

13 ลิ้นจี่
lín-jìi
lychee

14 ลำไย
lam-yai
longan

15 สตรอว์เบอร์รี่
sà-traw-berr-rîi
strawberry

16 องุ่น
à-ngùn
grape

48 ฉัน/ผมชอบกินผลไม้สด
Chǎn/Phǒm châwp gin phǒn-lá-mái sòt.
I love to eat fresh fruits.

17 แคนตาลูป
khaehn-taa-lúup
cantaloupe

18 พลับ
phláp
persimmon

19 แตงโม
taehng-moh
watermelon

20 ถั่วลิสง
thùa-lí-sŏng
peanuts

21 วอลนัต
wawl-nát
walnuts

22 พีแคน
phi-khaehr.
pecans

23 พิสตาชิโอ
phis-taa-chí-ôh
pistachios

24 อัลมอนด์
al-mâwn
almonds

26 แมคคาเดเมีย
make-khaa-deh-mĭa
macadamia nuts

27 เกาลัด
gao-lát
chestnuts

28 เฮเซลนัต
heh-sêhl-nát
hazel nuts

29 เมล็ดสน
má-lét-sŏn
pine nuts

25 เม็ดมะม่วงหิมพานต์
mét-má-mûang hĭm-má-phaan
cashew nuts

Additional Vocabulary

30 เมล็ดฟักทอง
má-lét fák-thawng
pumpkin seeds

31 เมล็ดแตงโม
má-lét taehng-moh
watermelon seeds

32 เมล็ดทานตะวัน
má-lét thaan-à-wan
sunflower seeds

33 งา
ngaa
sesame seeds

40 ธัญพืช
than-yá-phûeht
grains; cereals

41 ถั่ว
thùa
nuts

34 ข้าวโอ๊ต
khâaw óht
oats

35 ข้าวบาร์เลย์
khâaw baa-lêh
barley

36 ข้าวฟ่าง
khâaw fâang
millet

37 เมล็ดบักวีต
má-lét búk-wìit
buckwheat

38 ข้าว
khâaw
rice

39 ข้าวสาลี
khâaw săa-lii
wheat

42 ผลไม้แห้ง
phŏn-lá-mái hâehng
dried fruits

43 ถั่ว
thùa
beans

44 ข้าวโพด
khâaw-phôht
corn

45 แป้ง
pâehng
flour

46 น้ำผลไม้
náam phŏn-lá-mái
fruit juice

47 แพ้
pháeh
to be allergic; allergy

49 ขอสลัดอีกหนึ่งจานไม่ใส่ถั่วได้ไหม
Khăw sà-làt ìik nùeng jaan mâi-sài thùa dâi-mái?
Can I have one more salad without nuts?

50 คุณชอบถั่วอะไร
Khun châwp thùa à-rai?
What nuts do you like?

51 ฉัน/ผมชอบเม็ดมะม่วงหิมพานต์ แล้วคุณล่ะ
Chăn/Phŏm châwp mét-má-mûang hĭm-má-phaan. Láew khun lá?
I like cashew nuts. What about you?

52 ฉัน/ผมแพ้ถั่ว
Chăn/Phŏm pháeh thùa.
I am allergic to nuts.

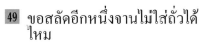
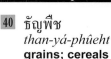

38

ไปตลาด
Pai tà-làat
At the market

1 เนื้อ
núea
meat

2 เนื้อวัว
núea wua
beef

3 ผักชี
phàk-chii
coriander leaves; cilantro

4 ผักชีฝรั่ง
phàk-chii fà-ràng
parsley

5 เนื้อหมู
núea mŭu
pork

6 เนื้อลูกแกะ; เนื้อแกะ
núea lûuk-gàe; núea gàe
lamb; mutton

7 โรสแมรี่
róhs-maeh-rîi
rosemary

8 เป็ด
pèt
duck

9 ไก่
gài
chicken

10 เลมอน
leh-mâwn
lemon

11 อาหารทะเล
aa-hăan thá-leh
seafood

12 ปลา
plaa
fish

13 ปลาหมึก
plaa-mùek
octopus

14 ผักชีลาว
phàk-chii lao
dill

15 กุ้ง
gûng
shrimp; prawns

16 ไข่
khài
eggs

17 ผัก
phàk
vegetables

18 คะน้า
khá-náa
kale

19 ผักกาดฮ่องเต้
phàk-gàat hâwng-têh
bok choy

20 กวางตุ้ง
gwaang-tûng
Chinese flowering cabbage

21 ปวยเล้ง
puay-léhng
spinach

22 ถั่วงอก
thùa-ngâwk
bean sprouts

58 ที่ประเทศไทย เราชอบซื้ออาหารที่ตลาดท้องถิ่น
Thîi prà-thêht Thai rao châwp súeh aa-hăan thîi tà-làat tháwng-thìn.
In Thailand, we like to buy our food at the local market.

59 ผักและเนื้อสัตว์สดมาก และถูกกว่าที่ซูเปอร์มาร์เก็ตนิดหน่อย
Phàk láe núea-sàt sòt mâak láe thùuk-gwàa thîi súp-pêrr-maa-gêt nít-nòy.
The vegetables and meat are very fresh there. And it is slightly cheaper than the supermarket.

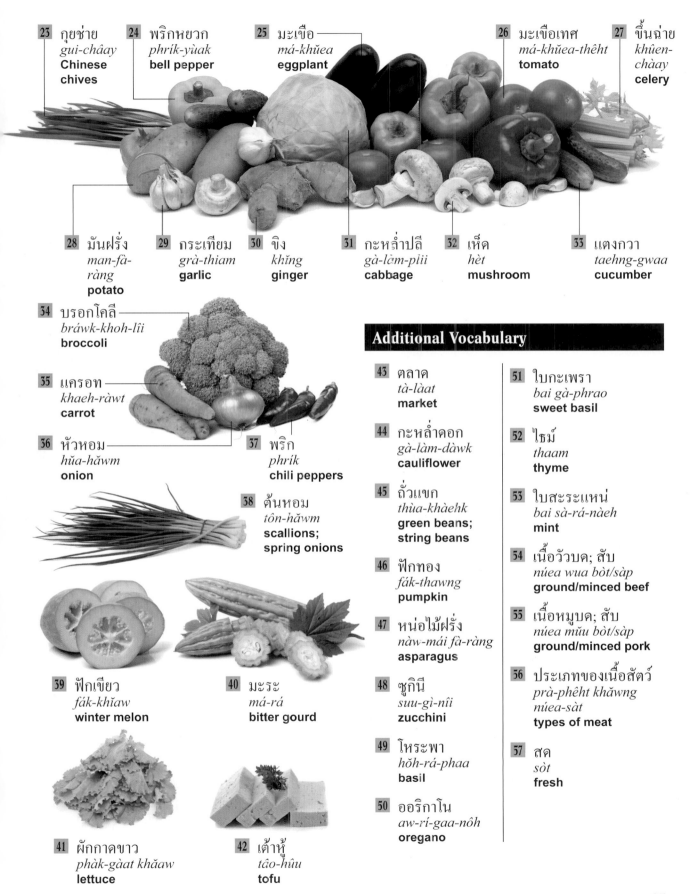

23 กุยช่าย
gui-châay
Chinese chives

24 พริกหยวก
phrík-yùak
bell pepper

25 มะเขือ
má-khŭea
eggplant

26 มะเขือเทศ
má-khŭea-thêht
tomato

27 ขึ้นฉ่าย
khûen-chàay
celery

28 มันฝรั่ง
man-fà-ràng
potato

29 กระเทียม
grà-thiam
garlic

30 ขิง
khĭng
ginger

31 กะหล่ำปลี
gà-làm-plii
cabbage

32 เห็ด
hèt
mushroom

33 แตงกวา
taehng-gwaa
cucumber

34 บรอกโคลี
bráwk-khoh-lîi
broccoli

35 แครอท
khaeh-ràwt
carrot

36 หัวหอม
hŭa-hăwm
onion

37 พริก
phrík
chili peppers

38 ต้นหอม
tôn-hăwm
scallions; spring onions

39 ฟักเขียว
fák-khĭaw
winter melon

40 มะระ
má-rá
bitter gourd

41 ผักกาดขาว
phàk-gàat khăaw
lettuce

42 เต้าหู้
tâo-hûu
tofu

Additional Vocabulary

43 ตลาด
tà-làat
market

44 กะหล่ำดอก
gà-làm-dàwk
cauliflower

45 ถั่วแขก
thùa-khàehk
green beans; string beans

46 ฟักทอง
fák-thawng
pumpkin

47 หน่อไม้ฝรั่ง
nàw-mái fà-ràng
asparagus

48 ซูกินี
suu-gì-nîi
zucchini

49 โหระพา
hŏh-rá-phaa
basil

50 ออริกาโน
aw-rí-gaa-nôh
oregano

51 ใบกะเพรา
bai gà-phrao
sweet basil

52 ไธม์
thaam
thyme

53 ใบสะระแหน่
bai sà-rá-nàeh
mint

54 เนื้อวัวบด; สับ
núea wua bòt/sàp
ground/minced beef

55 เนื้อหมูบด; สับ
núea mŭu bòt/sàp
ground/minced pork

56 ประเภทของเนื้อสัตว์
prà-phêht khăwng núea-sàt
types of meat

57 สด
sòt
fresh

60 เครื่องปรุง
khrûeang prung
seasonings

62 น้ำปลา
nám-plaa
fish sauce

61 ซอสถั่วเหลือง
sáwt thùa-lǔeang
soy sauce

63 ซอสพริก
sáwt phrík
chili sauce

64 น้ำมันงา
nám-man ngaa
sesame oil

65 น้ำมันมะกอก
nám-man má-gàwk
olive oil

66 น้ำมันหอย
nám-man hǒy
oyster sauce

70 อบเชย
òp-choei
cinnamon

67 พริกป่น
phrík pòn
chili powder

71 โป๊ยกั้ก
póhy-gák
star anise

68 พริกไทยป่น
phrík-thai pòn
ground pepper

69 เกลือ
gluea
salt

72 ขมิ้นป่น
khà-mîn pòn
ground turmeric

Additional Vocabulary

73 เต้าเจี้ยว
tâo-jîaw
soybean paste

74 น้ำส้มสายชู
náam-sôm sǎay-chuu
vinegar

75 น้ำตาล
náam-taan
sugar; candy

76 ไวน์สำหรับทำอาหาร
waai sǎm-ràp tham aa-hǎan
cooking wine

77 สาเก
sǎa-geh
rice wine

78 น้ำส้มสายชูหมักจากข้าว
náam-sôm sǎay-chuu màk jàak khâaw
rice vinegar

79 ผงพะโล้
phǒng phá-lóh
five-spice powder

80 ผงชูรส
phǒng chuu-rót
monosodium glutamate (MSG)

81 ผงกะหรี่
phǒng gà-rìi
curry powder

82 แป้ง
pâehng
starch

83 น้ำมันพืช
náam-man phûeht
cooking oil

84 น้ำมันถั่วลิสง
náam-man thùa-lí-sǒng
peanut oil

85 น้ำมันมะพร้าว
náam-man má-phráaw
coconut oil

86 น้ำมันปาล์ม
náam-man paam
palm oil

87 อาหารไทยทำง่ายถ้าคุณมีเครื่องปรุงครบทุกอย่าง
Aa-hǎan thai tham ngâay thâa khun mii khrûeang-prung khróp thúk-yàang.
Thai food is easy to cook once you have all the ingredients.

English-Thai Index

The following information is included for each entry–the English word, the Thai word and its romanisation, the section number and the order in which the word appeared in that section, followed by the page number where the word appears. For example:

English word	Thai word/Romanisation	Lesson and order	Page in book
happy	มีความสุข *mii khwaam-sùk*	[1–10]	86

88

[38–81] 86

curtain ผ้าม่าน *phâa-mâan* [3–17] 14

customs ศุลกากร *sŭn-lá-gaa-gawn* [31–23] 71

cute; adorable น่ารัก *nâa-rák* [29–31] 67

D

dance (performance art) เต้นรำ *tên-ram* [26–22] 61

dark color สีเข้ม *sĭi khêm* [7–15] 22

daughter ลูกสาว *lûuk săaw* [2–5] 12

daughter-in-law ลูกสะใภ้ *lûuk sà-phái* [2–32] 12

day วัน *wan* [16–4] 40

day of a month วันที่ *wan-thîi* [16–36] 41

debt หนี้ *nîi* [9–29] 27

decade (10 years) ทศวรรษ *thót-sà-wát* [16–37] 41

December ธันวาคม *than-waa-khom* [16–27] 41

decision ตัดสินใจ *tàt-sĭn-jai* [10–36] 29

delivery van รถตู้ส่งของ *rót-tûu sòng khǎwn* [12–7] 32

dentist ทันตแพทย์; หมอฟัน *than-tà-phâeht (formal); mǎw-fan (informal)* [25–14] 59

dentistry ทันตกรรม *than-tà-gam* [27–22] 63

depart ออก *àwk* [8–20] 25

department store ห้างสรรพสินค้า *hâawng sàp-phá-sĭn-kháa* [10–23] 29

dermatology ผิวหนังวิทยา *phĭw-nǎng wít-thá-yaa* [27–29] 63

desktop computer คอมพิวเตอร์ ตั้งโต๊ะ *khawm-phiw-têrr tâng tóh* [32–4] 54

desk โต๊ะ *tó* [3–36] 15

diary ไดอารี่ *dai-aa-rîi* [16–44] 41

dictionary พจนานุกรม *phòt-jà-naa-nú-grom* [19–12] 46

diet drinks เครื่องดื่มไม่มีน้ำตาล *khrûeang-dùehm mâi-mii náam-taan* [36–15] 80

difficult ยาก *yâak* [8–15] 25; [21–28] 51

digestive system ระบบย่อย อาหาร *rá-bòp yôy aa-hǎan* [4–37] 17

digits ตัวเลข *tua-lêhk* [5–29] 19

dill ผักชีลาว *phàk-chii lao* [38–14] 84

dinosaur ไดโนเสาร์ *dai-noh-sǎo* [29–10] 66

direction ทาง *thaang* [13–36] 35

discount ลด *lót* [9–24] 27

distance ระยะทาง *rá-yá-thaang* [13–37] 35

do not have ไม่มี *mâi mii* [8–16] 25

doctor หมอ; แพทย์ *mǎw (informal); phâeht (formal)* [27–4] 62

doctor's consultation room ห้อง ตรวจ *hâwng trùat* [27–18] 62

dog หมา *mǎa* [29–21] 67

donuts โดนัท *doh-nát* [35–5] 78

door ประตู *prà-tuu* [3–46] 15

down ลง *long* [8–1] 24

downtown ใจกลางเมือง *jai-glaang-mueang* [11–23] 31

dragon มังกร *mang-gawn* [29–23] 67

crawer ลิ้นชัก *lín-chák* [3–34] 15

cried fruits ผลไม้แห้ง *phǒn-lá-mái hâehng* [37–42] 83

crive a car ขับรถ *khàp rót* [12–24] 33

criver คนขับ *khon khàp* [12–3] 32

crums กลอง *glawng* [26–6] 60

cuck เป็ด *pèt* [38–8] 84

E

ear, nose, and throat หู จมูก และคอ *hǔu jà-mùuk láe khaw* [27–25] 63

ear หู *hǔu* [4–2] 16

early เช้า *cháo* [15–24] 39

early morning เช้าตรู่ *cháo-trùu* [15–18] 39

earphones หูฟัง *hǔu-fang* [26–27] 61

earth; ground พื้นดิน *phúehn din* [28–31] 65

east ทิศตะวันออก *thít tà-wan-àwk* [13–10] 34

East Timor ติมอร์ตะวันออก *tì-maw tà-wan-àwk* [32–12] 72

Easter วันอีสเตอร์ *wan iis-têrr* [18–19] 44

easy ง่าย *ngâay* [3–15] 25; [21–27] 51

economics เศรษฐศาสตร์ *sèht-thà-sàat* [19–37] 47

eggplant มะเขือ *má-khǔea* [38–25] 85

eggs ไข่ *khài* [38–16] 84

eight แปด *pàeht* [5–8] 18

eight pieces of clothing เสื้อผ้าแปดชุด *sûea-phâa pàeht chút* [22–5] 52

elbow ข้อศอก *khâw-sàwk* [4–20] 17

electric car รถยนต์ไฟฟ้า *rót-yon fai-fáa* [24–18] 54

electric socket; power point ปลั๊กไฟ *plák fai* [3–50] 14

elementary school โรงเรียนประถม ศึกษา *rohng-rian prà-thǒm sùek-sǎa* [20–33] 49

elephant ช้าง *cháang* [29–14] 67

elevator ลิฟต์ *líf* [3–45] 15

email อีเมล *ii-mehl* [23–15] 54

emergency ฉุกเฉิน *chùk-chěrrn* [27–39] 63

emergency room ห้องฉุกเฉิน *hâwng chùk-chěrrn* [27–2] 62

employee พนักงาน *phá-nák-ngaan* [25–26] 59

end จบ *jòp* [8–24] 25

energy drinks เครื่องดื่มชูกำลัง *khrûeang-dùehm chuu gam-lang* [36–16] 80

engineer วิศวกร *wít-sà-wá-gawn* [25–24] 58

English ภาษาอังกฤษ *Phaa-sǎa Ang-grìt* [33–1] 74

enter เข้า *khâo* [3–6] 24

enthusiastic กระตือรือร้น *grà-tueh-rueh-rón* [2–41] 12

entrepreneur ผู้ประกอบการ *phûu-prà-gàwp-gaan* [25–22] 59

environment สิ่งแวดล้อม *sìng-wâeht-láwm* [28–28] 65

equals เท่ากับ *thâo-gàp* [5–21] 19

eraser ยางลบ *yang-lóp* [19–14] 47

essay บทความ *bòt-khwaam* [21–16] 51

Europe ทวีปยุโรป *thá-wîip yú-ròhp* [23–16] 73

even numbers เลขคู่ *lêhk khûu* [5–25] 19

Everybody eats together. ทุกคนกิน อาหารด้วยกัน *Thúk khon gin aa-hǎan dûay gan.* [6–14] 21

exams สอบ *sàwp* [19–1] 46

exercise book หนังสือแบบฝึกหัด *nǎng-sǔeh baehp-fùek-hàt* [21–24] 51

exit ออก *àwk* [8–6] 24

expensive แพง *phaehng* [9–26] 27

expressway ทางด่วน *thaang-dùan* [11–18] 31

extraordinary พิเศษ *phí-sèt* [23–47] 55

extremely มากที่สุด *mâak thîi-sùt* [29–33] 67

eye ตา *taa* [4–8] 16

eyebrow คิ้ว *khíw* [4–7] 16

F

face หน้า *nâa* [4–5] 16

Facebook เฟซบุ๊ก *fét-búk* [24–18] 57

FaceTime เฟซไทม์ *fét-thaam* [24–21] 57

fake ปลอม *plawm* [8–27] 25

famous มีชื่อเสียง *mii chûeh sĭang* [26–32] 61

family ครอบครัว *khrâwp-khrua* [2–38] 12

fan พัด *phát* [17–15] 43

far ไกล *glai* [8–25] 25; [13–43] 45

farmer เกษตรกร; ชาวนา *gà-sèht-tà-gawn (formal); chaaw-naa (informal)* [25–20] 59

fast เร็ว *rew* [8–28] 25

fat อ้วน *ûan* [3–13] 25

father พ่อ *phâw* [2–13] 13

Father's Day วันพ่อ *wan phâw* [18–12] 44

father's elder brother ลุง *lung* [2–11] 13

father's older sister ป้า *pâa* [2–29] 12

father's younger brother/sister อา *aa* [2–28] 12

February กุมภาพันธ์ *gum-phaa-phan* [16–17] 41

female ผู้หญิง *phûu yĭng* [2–3] 12

festival; holiday เทศกาลวันหยุด *thêht-sà-gaan wan-yùt* [18–1] 44

fever ไข้ *khài* [27–12] 62

fifteen minutes past six หกโมงสิบ ห้านาที *hòk mohng sìp-hâa naa-thii* [15–8] 38

fifteen minutes to seven หกโมงสี่ สิบห้านาที *hòk mohng sìi-sìp-hâa naa-thii* [15–10] 38

file ไฟล์ *faay* [23–22] 55

finally ในที่สุด *nai-thîi-sùt* [15–36] 39

financier นักการเงิน *nák-gaan-ngerrn* [25–3] 58

fingers นิ้วมือ *níw mueh* [4–15] 16

finish line เส้นชัย *sêhn-chai* [30–16] 69

fire engine รถดับเพลิง *rót dàp-phlerrng* [12–16] 33

firefighter พนักงานดับเพลิง *phá-nák-ngaan dàp-phlerrng* [25–19] 59

fireworks พลุ; ดอกไม้ไฟ *phlú; dàwk-mái fai* [18–3] 44

first aid kit ชุดปฐมพยาบาล *chút pà-thǒm-phá-yaa-baan* [27–53] 63

fish ปลา *plaa* [29–28] 67; [38–12] 84

fish sauce น้ำปลา *nám-plaa* [38–62] 86

fitness gym ยิม; ฟิตเนส *yim; fít-nèt* [11–19] 31

five ห้า *hâa* [5–5] 18

five minutes past six หกโมงห้านาที *hòk mohng hâa naa-thii* [15–5] 38

five minutes to seven หกโมงห้าสิบ ห้านาที *hòk mohng hâa-sìp-hâa naa-thii* [15–11] 38

five tickets ตั๋วห้าใบ *tǔa hâa bai* [22–4] 52

five-spice powder ผงพะโล้ *phǒng phá-lóh* [38–79] 86

flashcards บัตรคำ *bàt kham* [21–32] 51

floor พื้น *phúehn* [3–16] 14

flour แป้ง *pâehng* [37–45] 83

flower ดอกไม้ *dàwk-mái* [28–2] 64

flute ขลุ่ย *khlùiy* [26–10] 60

fog หมอก *màwk* [14–25] 37

foot ฟุต *fút* [13–41] 35; เท้า *tháo* [4–23] 17

for the purpose of จุดประสงค์เพื่อ *jùt-prà-sŏng phûea* [28–34] 65

forehead หน้าผาก *nâa-phàak* [4–17] 16

forest ป่า *pàa* [28–14] 65

forgotten ลืมแล้ว *luehm láew* [8–23] 25

fork ส้อม *sâwm* [34–13] 76

former ก่อน *gàwn* [17–20] 43

four สี่ *sìi* [5–4] 18

four older brothers พี่ชายสี่คน *phîi-chaay sìi khon* [22–16] 53

four seasons สี่ฤดู *sìi rúe-duu* [17–19] 43

fraction เศษส่วน *sèht sùan* [5–24] 19

free wifi ไวไฟฟรี *waai-faai frii* [31–28] 71

French ภาษาฝรั่งเศส *Phaa-sǎa Fà-ràng-sèht* [33–2] 74

french fries มันฝรั่งทอด *man fà-ràng thâwt* [35–28] 79

frequently บ่อยๆ *bòy bòy* [15–33] 39

fresh สด *sòt* [38–57] 85

freshman year in college นักศึกษาปี หนึ่ง *nák-sùek-sǎa pii nùeng* [20–37] 49

Friday วันศุกร์ *wan-sùk* [16–14] 40

friends เพื่อน *phûean* [1–40] 11

fried noodle (pad Thai) ผัดไทย *phàt-thai* [34–5] 76

fried rice ข้าวผัด *khâaw phàt* [34–6] 76

from จาก *jàak* [27–43] 63

fruit juice น้ำผลไม้ *náam phǒn-lá-mái* [35–18] 79; [36–3] 80; [37–46] 83

(eat till) full อิ่ม *ìm* [8–19] 25

future อนาคต *à-naa-khót* [8–21] 25

G

garage โรงรถ *rohng rót* [3–56] 14

garbage truck รถขนขยะ *rót khǒn khà-yà* [12–6] 32

garden สวน *sǔan* [28–1] 64

garlic กระเทียม *grà-thiam* [38–29] 85

gas station; petrol station ปั๊มน้ำมัน *pám náam-man* [11–6] 30

gathering; meeting รวมกลุ่ม; พบปะ *ruam glum; phóp pà* [1–19] 11

general medicine อายุรกรรมทั่วไป *aa-yú-rá-gam thûa-pai* [27–23] 63

general surgery ศัลยกรรมทั่วไป *săn-yá-gam thûa-pai* [27–24] 63

generally โดยทั่วไป *dohy-thûa-pai* [10–34] 29

geography ภูมิศาสตร์ *phuum-mí-sàat* [19–43] 47

geometry เรขาคณิต *reh-khăa-khá-nít* [19–34] 47

German ภาษาเยอรมัน *Phaa-săa yerr-rá-man* [33–3] 74

Ghost Festival ผีตาโขน *phĭi-taa-khŏhn* [18–10] 44

gift ของขวัญ *khwăwng-khwan* [18–21] 45

ginger ขิง ใ*khĭng* [38–30] 85

giraffe ยีราฟ *yii-ráap* [29–3] 66

give ให้ *hâi* [8–2] 24

giving directions บอกทาง *bàwk thaang* [13–21] 34

glass; cup แก้ว *gâehw* [36–32] 81

glasses; spectacles แว่นตา *wâehn-taq* [10–11] 28

globe แผนที่โลก *phăehn-thîi lôhk* [32–28] 73

gloves ถุงมือ *thŭng-mueh* [14–31] 37

go ไป *pai* [8–17] 25

go faster ไปเร็วๆ *pai rew rew* [12–27] 33

go straight ตรงไป *trong pai* [12–29] 33; [13–31] 35

go to school ไปโรงเรียน *pai rohng-rian* [6–24] 20

go to work; get off work ไปทำงาน; เลิกงาน *pai tham-ngaan; lêrrk ngaan* [6–43] 20

goat แพะ *pháe* [29–11] 67

gold สีทอง *sĭi thawng* [7–13] 22

golf กอล์ฟ *gàwp* [30–17] 69

going to work ไปทำงาน *pai tham-ngaan* [25–24] 59

Google กูเกิล *guu-gêrrn* [24–19] 57

good ดี *dii* [8–7] 24

good weather อากาศดี *aa-gàat dii* [14–34] 37

gorilla กอริลลา *gaw-rin-lâa* [29–8] 66

Grab แกร็บ *gráehp* [12–36] 33

grade; class ชั้น **chán** *chán* [19–22] 47

grades เกรด *grèht* [20–22] 49

grains; cereals ธัญพืช *than-yá-phûeht* [37–40] 83

grammar ไวยากรณ์ *wai-yaa-gawn* [21–18] 51

grandson; granddaughter หลานชาย; หลานสาว *lăan-săaw; lăan chaay* [2–33] 12

grape องุ่น *à-ngùn* [37–16] 82

grass หญ้า *yâa* [28–5] 64

Greek ภาษากรีก *Phaa-săa Grìik* [33–10] 75

green สีเขียว *sĭi khĭaw* [7–7] 22

green beans; string beans ถั่วแขก *thùa-khàehk* [38–45] 85

green curry (usually sweet and mildly spicy) แกงเขียวหวาน

gaeng khĭaw wăan [34–16] 77

green papaya spicy salad ส้มตำ *sôm-tam* [34–20] 77

grey สีเทา *sĭi thao* [7–10] 22

grilled chicken ไก่ย่าง *gài-yâang* [34–21] 77

ground pepper พริกไทยป่น *phrík-thai pòn* [38–68] 86

ground turmeric ขมิ้นป่น *khà-mîn pòn* [38–72] 86

ground/minced beef เนื้อวัวบด; สับ *núea wua bòt/sàp* [38–54] 85

ground/minced pork เนื้อหมูบด; สับ *núea mŭu bòt/sàp* [38–55] 85

guest; customer ลูกค้า *lûuk kháa* [1–20] 11

guesthouse เกสต์เฮ้าส์ *gehs-háo* [11–20] 31; [31–25] 71

guitar กีต้าร์ *gii-tâa* [26–1] 60

gynecology นรีเวชวิทยา *ná-rii-wêht wit-thá-yaa* [27–27] 63

H

hail ลูกเห็บ *lûuk-hèp* [14–29] 37

hair ผม *phŏm* [4–6] 16

half past six หกโมงครึ่ง *hòk mohng khrûeng* [15–9] 38

Halloween วันฮาโลวีน *wan haa-loh-wiin* [18–18] 45

ham แฮม *haehm* [35–12] 78

hamburger แฮมเบอร์เกอร์ *haehm berr-gêrr* [37–27] 79

hand มือ *mueh* [4–18] 17

happy มีความสุข *mii khwaam-sùk* [1–10] 10; ดีใจ *dii-jai* [8–31] 25

Happy birthday! สุขสันต์วันเกิด *Sùk-săn wan-gèrrt!* [18–31] 45

hat หมวก *mùak* [10–16] 28; [13–30] 37

have มี *mii* [8–16] 25

hazel nuts เฮเซลนัต *heh-sêhl-nát* [37–28] 83

head หัว *hŭa* [4–1] 16

health สุขภาพ *sùk-khà-phâap* [4–47] 17

healthy แข็งแรง *khăeng-raehng* [30–30] 69

heart หัวใจ *hŭa-jai* [4–32] 17

Hebrew ภาษาฮิบรู *Phaa-săa Hí-bʉru* [33–11] 75

here ที่นี่ *thîi-nîi* [13–2] 34

high สูง *sŭung* [8–29] 25

high speed train รถไฟความเร็วสูง *rót-fai khwaam-rew sŭung* [12–8] 32

higher two-string fiddle ซอด้วง *saw-dûang* [26–4] 60

highlighter ปากกาไฮไลท์ *pàak-gaa hai-lái* [19–19] 47

Hindi ภาษาฮินดี *Phaa-săa Hin-dii* [33–13] 75

history ประวัติศาสตร์ *prà-wàt-sàat* [19–29] 47

hobby งานอดิเรก *ngaan à-dì-rèhk* [27–31] 61

home delivery ซื้อของออนไลน์ *súeh khăwng gwn-laay* [10–X] 29

homework การบ้าน *gaan-bâan* [19–27] 47

hope หวัง *wăng* [27–50] 63

horse ม้า *máa* [29–15] 67

horse carriage ม้า *rót-máa* [12–33] 33

hospital โรงพยาบาล *rohng phá-yaa-baan* [27–1] 62

hot ร้อน *ráwn* [14–20] 37

hot dog ฮอทดอก *háwt-dàwk* [35–1] 78

hot water น้ำร้อน *náam ráwn* [36–29] 81

hot weather อากาศร้อน *aa-gàat ráwn* [14–21] 37

hotel โรงแรม *rohng-raehm* [11–1] 30; [31–1] 70

hotel reservation การจองโรงแรม *gaan-jawng rohng-raehm* [31–24] 71

hour ชั่วโมง *chûa-mohng* [15–1] 38

house บ้าน *bâan* [3–51] 14; [11–26] 31

housefly แมลงวัน *má-laehng wan* [29–25] 67

how (wonderful, etc.) เหลือเกิน *lŭea-gerrn* [29–29] 67

How are things? เป็นยังไงบ้าง *Pen yang-ngai bâang?* [1–38] 11

How much is it? เท่าไรคะ *Thâo-rài khá?* [10–43] 29

how much longer? นานเท่าไร *naan thâo-rài* [13–56] 35

however อย่างไรก็ตาม *yàang-rai gâw-taam* [28–39] 65

hungry หิว *hĭw* [8–19] 25

hurricane พายุเฮอร์ริเคน *phaa-yú herr-rí-khehn* [14–38] 37

hurts บาดเจ็บ *bàat-jèp* [27–40] 63

husband สามี *săa-mii* [2–27] 12

husband and wife สามี กับ ภรรยา *săa-mii gàp phan-yaa* [2–14] 13

I

I; me ฉัน; ผม *chăn (female); phŏm (male)* [2–20] 13

ice cream ไอศกรีม; ไอติม *ai-sà-khriim (formal); ai-tim (informal)* [35–7] 78

ice cubes น้ำแข็งก้อน *náam khăeng gâwn* [36–31] 81

ice-skating สเก็ตน้ำแข็ง *sà-gét náam-khăeng* [30–18] 69

iced tea ชาเย็น *chaa-yen* [36–8] 80

idiom สำนวน *săm-nuan* [21–10] 51

idle ว่าง *wâang* [8–8] 24

if ถ้า *thâa* [28–41] 65

illness ไม่สบาย *mâi sà-baay* [4–48] 17

immediately เดี๋ยวนี้ *dĭaw-níi* [13–57] 35

important สำคัญ *săm-khan* [27–51] 63

in a moment อีกแป๊บเดียว; อีกสักครู่ *ìik páep-diaw (informal); ìik sàk-khrûu (formal)* [15–34] 39

in addition นอกจากนี้ *nâwk-jàak-níi* [23–46] 55

in front ข้างหน้า *khâang-nâa* [13–14] 34

in the afternoon; p.m. ตอนบ่าย *tawn-bàay* [15–21] 39

in the morning; a.m. ตอนเช้า *tawn-cháa* [15–19] 39

index ดัชนี *dàt-chá-nii* [28–25] 65

India อินเดีย *in-dia* [32–25] 73

Indonesia อินโดนีเซีย *in-doh-nii-sia* [32–11] 72

Indonesian ภาษาอินโดนีเซีย *Phaa-săa In-doh-nii-sia* [33–14] 75

injection ฉีดยา *chìit-yaa* [27–17] 62

inside ข้างใน *khâang nai* [8–22] 25; [13–34] 35

Instagram อินสตาแกรม *in-sà-taa-graem* [24–17] 57

installment (payment) ค่างวด *khâa-ngûat* [9–33] 27

intelligent; clever ฉลาด *chà-làat* [20–23] 49

interest ดอกเบี้ย *dàwk-bîa* [9–27] 27

internet access เข้าอินเทอร์เน็ต *khâo in-terr-nèt* [23–28] 55

internet cafes ร้านอินเตอร์เน็ต *ráan in-terr-nèt* [24–4] 56

internet language ภาษาอินเทอร์เน็ต *phaa-săa in-terr-nèt* [24–26] 56

Internet slang ภาษาสแลงใน อินเทอร์เน็ต *phaa-săa sà-laehng nai in-terr-nèt* [24–28] 56

intestines ลำไส้ *lam-sâi* [4–34] 17

introduce yourself แนะนำตัว *náe-nam tua* [1–14] 11

it มัน *man* [29–32] 67

Italian ภาษาอิตาลี *Phaa-săa Ì-taa-lîi* [33–5] 74

Italy อิตาลี *ì-taa-lîi* [32–27] 73

J

January มกราคม *mók-gà-raa-khom* [16–16] 41

Japan ญี่ปุ่น *yîi-pùn* [32–21] 73

Japanese ภาษาญี่ปุ่น *Phaa-săa Yîi-pùn* [33–8] 74

jasmine blossoms ดอกมะลิ *dàwk má-lí* [17–8] 42

jeans กางเกงยีนส์ *gaang-gehng yii* [10–9] 28

judge ผู้พิพากษา *phûu-phi-phâak-săa* [25–2] 58

June มิถุนายน *mí-thù-naa-yon* [16–21] 41

July กรกฎาคม *gà-rá-gà-daa-khom* [16–22] 41

junior year in college นักศึกษาปีสาม *nák-sùek-săa pii săam* [20–39] 49

joyful สนุก *sà-nùk* [1–11] 10

K

kale คะน้า *khá-náa* [38–18] 84

karaoke คาราโอเกะ *khaa-raa-oh-gè* [26–11] 61

ketchup; tomato sauce ซอสมะเขือเทศ *sáwt má-khŭea-thêht* [35–36] 79

kettle กาน้ำร้อน *gaa náam ráwn* [3–29] 15

keys กุญแจ *gun-jaeh* [3–5] 14

keyboard แป้นพิมพ์; คีย์บอร์ด *pâehn phim; khii-bàwt* [23–5] 54

kidneys ไต *tai* [4–33] 17

kilometer กิโลเมตร *gì-loh-méht* [13–38] 35

kitchen ห้องครัว *hâwng khrua* [3–23] 15

knee เข่า *khào* [4–21] 17

knife มีด *mîit* [34–14] 76

Korea เกาหลี *gao-lĭi* [32–22] 73

odd numbers เลขคี่ lêhk khîi [5–26] 19

of course แน่นอน nâeh-nawn [28–40] 65

office สำนักงาน săm-nák-ngaan [25–15] 58

office water dispenser ตู้กดน้ำ tûu gòt náam [36–28] 81

oil น้ำมัน náam-man [28–22] 65

ointment ยาทา yaa-thaa [27–37] 63

old เก่า gào [8–4] 24; แก่ gàeh [8–10] 25

older brother พี่ชาย phîi-chaay [2–19] 13

older sister พี่สาว phîi-săaw [2–18] 13

olive oil น้ำมันมะกอก nám-man má-gàwk [38–65] 86

omelet with minced pork ไข่เจียวหมูสับ khài-jiaw mŭu-sàp [34–23] 77

on a coach บนรถทัวร์ bon rót-thua [31–12] 70

on a cruise บนเรือสำราญ bon ruea săm-raan [31–11] 70

on sale ลดราคา lót raa-khaa [10–21] 29

oncology มะเร็งวิทยา má-reng wít-thá-yaa [27–30] 63

one หนึ่ง nùeng [5–1] 18

one bowl of soup แกงหนึ่งถ้วย gaehng nùeng thûay [22–6] 52

one chair เก้าอี้หนึ่งตัว gâo-îi nùeng tua [22–8] 52

one half ครึ่ง khrûeng [5–11] 18

one pair of shoes รองเท้าหนึ่งคู่ rawng-tháo nùeng khûu [22–3] 52

one quarter หนึ่งส่วนสี่ nùeng sùan sìi [5–13] 18

one side ข้างหนึ่ง khâang nùeng [13–52] 35

one third หนึ่งส่วนสาม nùeng sùan săam [5–14] 18

onion หัวหอม hŭa-hăwm [38–36] 85

online ออนไลน์ awn-laai [23–32] 55

online friends เพื่อนออนไลน์ phûean awn-laai [24–2] 56

online search ค้นหาออนไลน์ khôn-hăa awn-laai [23–40] 55

online shopping ซื้อของออนไลน์ súeh-khăwng awn-laay [10–29] 29; [24–3] 56

open เปิด pèrrt [8–12] 25

operating system ระบบปฏิบัติการ rá-bòp pà-tì-bàt-gaan [23–20] 55

ophthalmology จักษุวิทยา jàk-sù wít-thá-yaa [27–28] 63

opportunity โอกาส oh-gàat [25–32] 59

opposite ตรงข้าม trong-khâam [13–44] 35

orange (color) สีส้ม sĭi sôm [7–11] 22

orange ส้ม sôm [37–3] 82

orange juice น้ำส้ม náam sôm [36–4] 80

orchestra วงออเคสตรา wong aw-khes-tráa [26–30] 61

oregano ออริกาโน aw-rí-gaa-nôh [38–50] 85

organs อวัยวะ à-wai-yá-wá [4–36] 17

other อื่น ùehn [10–37] 29

outside ข้างนอก khâang nâwk [8–22] 25

outside ข้างนอก khâang-nâwk [13–33] 35

oven เตาอบ tao-òp [3–27] 15

overcast มืดครึ้ม mûeht khrúem [14–6] 36

oyster sauce น้ำมันหอย nám-man hŏy [38–66] 86

P

painting ภาพวาด phâap wâat [3–6] 14

palm oil น้ำมันปาล์ม náam-man paam [38–86] 86

pancakes แพนเค้ก phaehn-khéhk [35–33] 79

panda หมีแพนด้า mĭi phaehn-dâa [29–9] 66

papaya มะละกอ má-lá-gaw [37–10] 82

paper currency ธนบัตร; แบงค์ thá-ná-bàt (formal); báehng (informal) [9–2] 26

parents พ่อแม่ phâw mâeh [2–6] 12

park สวนสาธารณะ sŭan săa-thaa-rá-ná [28–3] 64

parsley ผักชีฝรั่ง phàk-chii fà-ràng [38–4] 84

passenger ผู้โดยสาร phûu-dohy-săan [12–19] 33

passport หนังสือเดินทาง năng-sŭeh derr-thaang [31–7] 70

password รหัสผ่าน rá-hàt phàan [23–17] 55

(in the) past แต่ก่อน tàeh-gàwn [15–32] 39

past อดีต à-dìit [8–21] 25

pasta; spaghetti พาสต้า; สปาเก็ตตี้ pháas-tâa; sà-paa-gét-tîi [35–4] 78

paternal grandfather ปู่ pùu [2–7] 13

paternal grandmother ย่า yâa [2–8] 13

patient คนไข้ khon khâi [27–5] 62

peach ลูกพีช lûuk phiit [37–9] 82

peacock นกยูง nók-yuung [29–18] 67

peanut oil น้ำมันถั่วลิสง náam-man thùa-lí-sŏng [38–84] 86

peanuts ถั่วลิสง thùa-lí-sŏng [37–20] 83

pear ลูกแพร์; สาลี่ lûuk phaeh; săa-lìi [37–5] 82

pecans พีแคน phi-khaehn [37–22] 83

pedestrian คนเดินถนน khon derrn thà-nŏn [11–34] 31

pedestrian crossing ทางม้าลาย thaang máa-laay [11–35] 31

pediatrics กุมารเวชศาสตร์ gù-maan wêht-chá-sàat [27–26] 63

pedicab; trishaw รถสามล้อ rót săam-láw [12–18] 33

pen ปากกา pàak-gaa [19–13] 47

pencil ดินสอ din-săw [19–20] 47

pencil sharpener กบเหลาดินสอ gòp lăo din-săw [19–16] 47

percent (%) เปอร์เซ็นต์ perr-sen [5–23] 19

perhaps บางที bang-thii [34–32] 77

persimmon พลับ phláp [37–18] 82

pertaining to เกี่ยวข้องกับ gìaw-khâwng gàp [27–49] 63

pharmacist เภสัชกร pheh-sàt-chá-gawn [25–6] 58

Philippines ฟิลิปปินส์ fi-lip-pin [32–5] 72

phone charger สายชาร์จโทรศัพท์ săay cháat thoh-rá-sàp [24–30] 56

photocopier เครื่องถ่ายเอกสาร khrûeang thàay-èhk-gà-săan [20–7] 48

photograph รูปถ่าย rûup-thàay [31–15] 70

photographer ช่างภาพ châang-phâap [25–12] 59

phrase คำพูด kham-phûut [21–12] 51

physical education พละ phá-lá [19–5] 46

physiotherapy กายภาพบำบัด gaay-yá-phâap bam-bàt [27–31] 63

physics ฟิสิกส์ fí-sìk [19–39] 47

piano เปียโน pia-noh [26–8] 60

pills ยาเม็ด yaa-mét [27–16] 62

pilot นักบิน nák-bin [25–13] 59

pillow หมอน măwn [3–19] 14

pine nuts เมล็ดสน má-lét-sŏn [37–29] 83

pineapple สับปะรด sàp-pà-rót [37–8] 82

pink สีชมพู sĭi chom-phuu [7–12] 22

pistachios พิสตาชิโอ phis-taa-chi-ôh [37–23] 83

pizza พิซซ่า phít-sâa [35–3] 78

place สถานที่ sà-thăan-thîi [13–51] 35

plane ticket ตั๋วเครื่องบิน tŭa khrûeang-bin [31–19] 71

plant พืช phûeht [28–19] 65

plate จาน jaan [34–12] 76

play basketball เล่นบาสเก็ตบอล lêhn báas-gét-bawn [30–26] 69

poem กลอน glawn [21–15] 51

police station สถานีตำรวจ sà-thăa-nii tam-rùat [11–17] 31

pollution มลพิษ mon-lá-phít [28–4] 64

pop group นักร้องเพลงป๊อป nák-ráwng phleng páwp [26–19] 61

pop music เพลงป๊อป phleng páwp [26–25] 61

pork เนื้อหมู núea mŭu [38–5] 84

ports พอร์ต phàwt [23–14] 54

Portuguese ภาษาโปรตุเกส Phaa-săa Proh-tù-gèht [33–18] 75

position ตำแหน่ง tam-nàehng [25–33] 59

post office ไปรษณีย์ prai-sà-nii [11–16] 31

postcard โปสการ์ด; ไปรษณียบัตร póht-sà-gáat (informal); prai-sà-nii-yá-bàt [31–31] 71

potato มันฝรั่ง man-fà-ràng [38–28] 85

potted plant ไม้กระถาง mái grà-thăang [3–47] 15

practice writing Thai alphabets หัดเขียนตัวอักษรไทย hàt khĭan tua àk-săwn Thai [21–36] 51

prescription ใบสั่งยา bai-sàng-yaa [27–35] 63

price ราคา raa-khaa [9–23] 27

principal ครูใหญ่ khruu yài [20–17] 49

private school โรงเรียนเอกชน rohng-rian èhk-gà-chon [20–29] 49

professor; lecturer อาจารย์ aa-jaan [20–10] 48

program รายการ raay-gaan [26–24] 61

public bus รถเมล์ rót-meh [12–12] 33

public school โรงเรียนรัฐบาล rohng-rian rát-thà-baan [20–30] 49

pudding พุดดิ้ง phút-dîng [35–8] 78

pumpkin ฟักทอง fák-thawng [38–46] 85

pumpkin seeds เมล็ดฟักทอง má-lét fák-thawng [37–30] 83

punctual ตรงเวลา trong weh-laa [15–23] 39

purple สีม่วง sĭi mûang [7–8] 22

purpose เป้าหมาย pâo-măay [19–50] 47

put on ใส่ sài [8–14] 25

Q

quarter (hour) สิบห้านาที sìp-hâa naa-thii [15–7] 38

quiet เงียบ ngîap [28–10] 64

R

racket ไม้ mái [30–25] 69

radiology รังสีวิทยา rang-sĭi wít-thá-yaa [27–33] 63

railing ราวระเบียง raaw rá-biang [3–3] 14

rain ฝน fŏn [14–10] 36

raincoat เสื้อกันฝน sûea gan-fŏn [14–2] 36

raining ฝนตก fŏn tòk [14–11] 36

rainstorm พายุฝน phaa-yú fŏn [14–28] 37

rainy ฤดูฝน rúe-duu fŏn [17–5] 42

raise your hand ยกมือ yók mueh [20–9] 48

range hood; cooker hood เครื่องดูดควัน khrûeang dùut khwan [3–28] 15

reading อ่านหนังสือ àan năng-sŭeh [19–2] 46

real จริง jing [8–27] 25

receipt ใบเสร็จ bai-sèt [9–32] 27

receive รับ ráp [8–2] 24

recycling การรีไซเคิล gaan rii-sai-khêrrn [28–20] 65

red สีแดง sĭi daehng [7–2] 22

red curry paste with chicken พะแนงไก่ phá-naeng gài [34–18] 77

red wine ไวน์แดง waai-daehng [36–19] 81

refrigerator ตู้เย็น tûu yen [3–26] 15

refund คืนเงิน khuehn ngerrn [10–42] 29

relatives ญาติ yâat [2–34] 12

remembered จำได้ jam dâi [8–23] 25

respiratory system ระบบหายใจ rá-bòp prà-sàat [4–38] 17

restaurant ร้านอาหาร ráan aa-hăan [31–38] 71

return คืน khuehn [8–30] 25

rice ข้าว khâaw [37–38] 83

rice wine สาเถ sŭa-geh [38–77] 86

rice vinegar น้ำส้มสายชูหมักจาก ข้าว náam-sôm săay-chuu màk jàak khâaw [38–78] 86

ride a bike ขี่จักรยาน khìi jàk-grà-yaan [12–25] 33

ride a train นั่งรถไฟ nâng rót-fai [12–23] 33

right ถูก thùuk [8–26] 25

right side ข้างขวา khâang-khwăa [13–27] 35

river แม่น้ำ mâeh-náam [28–8] 64

road ถนน thà-nŏn [11–38] 31

Rocket Festival บุญบั้งไฟ bun-

bâng-fai [18–8] 44
roof หลังคา lăng-khaa [3–53] 14
room ห้อง hâwng [3–22] 14
rosemary โรสแมรี่ róhs-maeh-rîi [38–7] 84
roses ดอกกุหลาบ dàwk-gù-làap [18–16] 45
rowing พายเรือ phaay-ruea [30–20] 69
rugby รักบี้ rák-bîi [30–3] 68
ruler ไม้บรรทัด mái ban-thát [19–17] 47
running วิ่ง wîng [30–11] 68
Russian ภาษารัสเซีย Phaa-săa Rát-sia [33–3] 74

S

sandwich แซนด์วิช saehn-wít [35–2] 78
S size ไซส์เอส sái S [7–31] 23
sad เสียใจ sĭa-jai [8–31] 25
salad สลัด sà-làt [35–13] 78
salt เกลือ gluea [38–69] 86
same; identical เหมือนกัน mŭean-gan [29–34] 67
sand break แผงกันทราย phăehng gân saay [28–13] 65
Santa Claus ซานตาคลอส saan-taa-khláwt [18–23] 45
satang (coin) สตางค์ sà-taang [9–5] 26
satisfied ดีใจ dii-jai [1–9] 10
Saturday วันเสาร์ wan-săo [16–15] 30
sausage ไส้กรอก sâi-gràwk [35–16] 78
savings เงินเก็บ ngerrn gèp [9–19] 27
scallions; spring onions ต้นหอม tôn-hăwm [38–38] 85
scarf ผ้าพันคอ phâa phan-khaw [10–20] 29
school โรงเรียน rohng-rian [20–16] 49
school holidays ปิดเทอม pìt-therrm [18–26] 45
school is over โรงเรียนเลิก rohng-rian lêrrk [6–25] 20
science วิทย์เทอม pìt-therrm [19–35] 47; [20–12] 48
scissors กรรไกร gan-grai [19–21] 47
screen หน้าจอ nâa-jaw [23–2] 54
seafood อาหารทะเล aa-hăan thá-leh [38–11] 84
seasonings เครื่องปรุง khrûeang prung [38–62] 86
secretary เลขานุการ leh-khăa-nú-gaan [25–18] 58
second วินาที wí-naa-thii [15–3] 38
self ตัวเอง tua-ehng [2–39] 12
selfie เซลฟี่ sehl-fîi [24–14] 57
senior high school โรงเรียนมัธยมศึกษาตอนปลาย rohng-rian mát-thá-yom sùek-săa tawn-plaay [20–35] 49
senior year in college นักศึกษาปีสี่ nák-sùek-săa pii sìi [20–40] 49
sentence ประโยค prà-yòhk [21–11] 51
September กันยายน gan-yaa-yon [16–24] 41
service provider ผู้ให้บริการ phûu hâi baw-rí-gaan [25–30] 59
sesame oil น้ำมันงา nám-man ngaa [38–64] 86
sesame seeds งา ngaa [37–33] 83
seven เจ็ด jèt [5–7] 18

Seven continents of the world เจ็ดทวีปในโลก jèt thá-wîip nai lôhk [32–13] 73
several times หลายครั้ง lăay khráng [27–44] 63
several bicycles จักรยานหลายคัน jàk-grà-yaan lăay khan [22–17] 53
shake hands เชคแฮนด์ chéhk haehn [1–28] 11
shape รูปทรง rûup song [7–38] 23
sheep แกะ gàe [29–12] 67
shift work ทำงานเป็นกะ tham-ngaan pen gà [25–28] 59
ship; boat เรือ ruea [12–14] 33
shirt เสื้อเชิ้ต sûea-chérrt [10–14] 28
shoes รองเท้า rawng-tháo [10–13] 28
shop ร้าน ráan [10–22] 29; [11–3] 30
shopping center; mall ศูนย์การค้า; ห้าง sŭun-gaan-kháa; hâang [11–22] 31
shop staff พนักงานขาย phá-nák-ngaan khăay [10–25] 29
shopping bag ถุงช็อปปิ้ง thŭng cháwp-pîng [10–4] 28
short เตี้ย tîa [8–5] 24; สั้น sân [8–9] 24
short essay บทความย่อ bòt-khwaam yâw [21–14] 51
shoulder ไหล่ lài [4–24] 17
shower ฝักบัว fàk-bua [3–41] 15
shrimp; prawns กุ้ง gûng [38–15] 84
side ข้าง khâang [13–49] 35
sidewalk ทางเดิน thaang-derrn [11–28] 31
sightseeing ชมวิว chom-view [31–30] 71
silver สีเงิน sĭi ngerrn [7–14] 22
SIM card ซิมการ์ด sim gáat [24–34] 56
simple พื้นฐาน phúehn-thăan [21–25] 51
Singapore สิงคโปร์ sĭng-khá-poh [32–10] 72
singer นักร้อง nák-ráwng [26–13] 61
sink อ่างล้างหน้า àang láang nâa [3–40] 15
sister-in-law น้องสะใภ้; พี่สะใภ้ náwng sà-phái; phîi sà-phái [2–37] 12
sisters พี่สาวน้องสาว phîi-săaw náwng-săaw [2–16] 13
six หก hòk [5–6] 18
six bowls of rice ข้าวหกถ้วย khâaw hòk thûay [22–14] 53
size ไซส์; ขนาด sái; khà-nàat [7–39] 23
skeletal system ระบบโครงกระดูก rá-bòp khrohng grà-dùuk [4–40] 17
skiing เล่นสกี lêhn sà-gii [30–19] 69
skin ผิวหนัง phĭw năng [4–41] 17
skinny ผอม phăwm [8–13] 25
skirt กระโปรง grà-prohng [10–8] 28
skyscraper ตึกสูง tùek-sŭung [11–12] 30
slow ช้า cháa [8–28] 25
slow down ช้าลง cháa long [12–26] 33
small เล็ก lék [7–37] 23; [8–11] 25
small change เงินย่อย ngerrn yôy [9–17] 27
smaller เล็กกว่า lék gwàa [7–41] 23
smartphone สมาร์ทโฟน sà-máat-

fohn [24–1] 56
smartwatch สมาร์ทวอทช์ sà-máat-wáwt [15–14] 39
smile ยิ้ม yím [1–31] 11
snake งู nguu [29–17] 67
sneakers รองเท้าผ้าใบ rawng-tháo phâa-bai [30–28] 69
snow หิมะ hì-má [14–15] 36
snowball fights ปาก้อนหิมะ paa gâwn hì-má [17–16] 43
social studies สังคมศึกษา săng-khom sùek-săa [19–36] 47
socks ถุงเท้า thŭng-tháo [10–12] 28
sodas โซดา soh-daa [36–27] 81
sofa โซฟา soh-faa [3–15] 14
software ซอฟต์แวร์ sáwp-waeh [23–19] 55
solar energy พลังงานแสงอาทิตย์ phá-lang-ngaan săehng-aa-thít [28–9] 64
son ลูกชาย lûuk chaay [2–1] 12
son-in-law ลูกเขย lûuk-khŏei [2–31] 12
sophomore year in college นักศึกษาปีสอง nák-sùek-săa pii săwng [20–38] 49
sound เสียง sĭang [6–18] 20
soup น้ำซุป; แกง náam súp (no meat); gaehng (with meat) [34–26] 77
south ทิศใต้ thít tâi [13–13] X
South America ทวีปอเมริกาใต้ thá-wîip à-meh-rí-gaa tâi [32–15] 73
southeast ทิศตะวันออกเฉียงใต้ thít tà-wan-àwk chĭang tâi [13–12] 34
southwest ทิศตะวันตกเฉียงใต้ thít tà-wan-tòk chĭang tâi [13–11] 34
souvenir shop ร้านขายของที่ระลึก ráan khăay khăwng-thîi-rá-lúek [31–13] 70
soy milk นมถั่วเหลือง nom thùa-lŭeang [36–9] 80
soy sauce ซอสถั่วเหลือง sáwt thùa-lŭeang [38–61] 86
soybean paste เต้าเจี้ยว tâo-jîaw [38–73] 86
Spanish ภาษาสเปน Phaa-săa Sà-pehn [33–6] 74
special พิเศษ phí-sèht [34–30] 77
spicy shrimp soup ต้มยำกุ้ง tôm-yam gûng [34–17] 77
spinach ป่วยเล้ง puay-léhng [38–21] 84
spoon ช้อน cháwn [34–15] 76
sports กีฬา gii-laa [30–8] 68
sports car รถสปอร์ต rót sà-pàwt [12–10] 32
sports drinks เครื่องดื่มเกลือแร่ khrûeang-dùehm gluea-râeh [36–17] 80
sports shirt; sweatshirt เสื้อกีฬา sûea gii-laa [30–27] 69
sports shoes รองเท้ากีฬา rawng-tháo gii-laa [30–21] 69
spring ฤดูใบไม้ผลิ rúe-duu bai-mái-phlì [17–1] 42
sprint วิ่งเร็วระยะสั้น wîng rew rá-yá-sân [30–10] 68
stadium สนามกีฬา sà-năam gii-laa [11–15] 31
star anise โป๊ยกั๊ก póhy-gák [38–71] 86

starch แป้ง pâehng [38–82] 86
steak สเต็ก sà-ték [35–15] 78
sticky rice ข้าวเหนียว khâaw-nĭaw [34–22] 77
stomach ท้อง tháwng [4–49] 17
stopwatch นาฬิกาจับเวลา naa-li-gaa jàp-weh-laa [15–13] 39
story เรื่อง rûeang [19–31] 47
stove เตา tao [3–31] 15
strange แปลก plàehk [29–38] 67
strawberry สตรอว์เบอร์รี่ sà-traw-berr-rîi [37–15] 82
street ถนน thà-nŏn [11–4] 30
street corner หัวมุมถนน hŭa-mum thà-nŏn [11–30] 31
strong signal สัญญาณแรง săn-yaan raehng [24–12] 57
student นักเรียน; นักศึกษา nák-rian (school); nák-sùek-săa (university) [20–15] 48
study room ห้องทำงาน hâwng tham-ngaan [3–2] 15
study time ทำการบ้าน tham gaan-bâan [6–34] 20
suburb นอกเมือง nâwk-mueang [11–25] 31
subway รถไฟใต้ดิน rót-fai tâi-din [12–11] 22
sudden ทันที than-thii [15–35] 39
sugar; candy น้ำตาล náam-taan [38–75] 86
summer ฤดูร้อน rúe-duu ráwn [17–2] 42
sun พระอาทิตย์ phrá-aa-thít [14–26] 37
sun shade ที่บังแดด thîi bang-dàeht [17–11] 42
sunblock lotion ครีมกันแดด khriim gan dàeht [17–17] 43
Sunday วันอาทิตย์ wan aa-thít [16–5] 40; [16–9] 40
sunflower seeds เมล็ดทานตะวัน má-lét thaan-tà-wan [37–32] 83
sunny side up eggs ไข่ดาวไม่สุก khài-daaw mâi sùk [35–21] 79
sunny weather แดดร้อน dàeht ráwn [14–36] 37
supermarket ซูเปอร์มาร์เก็ต súp-pêrr-maa-gét [11–5] 30
surname นามสกุล naam-sà-gun [1–24] 11
sweater เสื้อไหมพรม sûea măi-phrom [14–19] 37
sweet basil ใบกะเพรา bai gà-phrao [38–51] 85
swimming ว่ายน้ำ wâay-náam [30–21] 69

T

table โต๊ะ tó [3–14] 14
table lamp โคมไฟตั้งโต๊ะ khohm-fai tâng tó [3–33] 15
table tennis ปิงปอง ping-pawng [30–1] 68
tablet แท็บเล็ต táep-lèt [23–3] 54
Tagalog ภาษาตากาล็อก Phaa-săa Taa-gaa-láwk [33–17] 75
take off ถอด thàwt [8–14] 25
take a bus; by bus นั่งรถเมล์ nâng

Published by Tuttle Publishing, an imprint of Periplus
Editions (HK) Ltd

www.tuttlepublishing.com

ISBN: 978-0-8048-5218-0

25 24 23 22   10 9 8 7 6 5 4 3
Printed in China   2201EP

"Books to Span the East and West"

Tuttle Publishing was founded in 1832 in the small
New England town of Rutland, Vermont [USA]. Our
core values remain as strong today as they were
then—to publish best-in-class books which bring
people together one page at a time. In 1948, we
established a publishing office in Japan—and Tuttle
is now a leader in publishing English-language books
about the arts, languages and cultures of Asia. The
world has become a much smaller place today and
Asia's economic and cultural influence has grown.
Yet the need for meaningful dialogue and information
about this diverse region has never been greater. Over
the past seven decades, Tuttle has published thousands
of books on subjects ranging from martial arts and
paper crafts to language learning and literature–and
our talented authors, illustrators, designers and
photographers have won many prestigious awards.
We welcome you to explore the wealth of information
available on Asia at **www.tuttlepublishing.com.**

Distributed by

**North America, Latin America &
Europe**
Tuttle Publishing
364 Innovation Drive
North Clarendon,
VT 05759-9436 U.S.A.
Tel: 1 (802) 773-8930
Fax: 1 (802) 773-6993
info@tuttlepublishing.com
www.tuttlepublishing.com

Japan
Tuttle Publishing
Yaekari Building, 3rd Floor
5-4-12 Osaki
Shinagawa-ku
Tokyo 141-0032
Tel: (81) 3 5437-0171
Fax: (81) 3 5437-0755
sales@tuttle.co.jp
www.tuttle.co.jp

Asia Pacific
Berkeley Books Pte. Ltd.
3 Kallang Sector #04-01/02
Singapore 349278
Tel: (65) 6741-2178
Fax: (65) 6741-2179
inquiries@periplus.com.sg
www.tuttlepublishing.com

TUTTLE PUBLISHING® is a registered trademark of Tuttle Publishing, a division of Periplus Editions (HK) Ltd.

**The free online audio recordings for this book
may be downloaded as follows:**

Type the following URL into your web browser:
www.tuttlepublishing.com/Thai-Picture-Dictionary
For support, email us at info@tuttlepublishing.com

Photo Credits

ตึกสูง
tùek-sǔung
skyscrapers

ตลาดน้ำ
tà-làat-náam
floating market

บาท
bàat (Baht)
**the official currency
of Thailand**

ทุเรียน
thú-rian
durian

สงกรานต์
sǒng-graan
(Songkran) Water festival